I0155988

Captain Gronow's Military Reminiscences

Captain R. H. Gronow

Captain Gronow's Military Reminiscences

With the First Guards During the Later Peninsular
War and the Waterloo Campaign, 1813-15

ILLUSTRATED

Written by Himself
Edited by John H. Lewis

LEONAUR

Captain Gronow's Military Reminiscences
With the First Guards During the Later Peninsular War and the Waterloo Campaign,
1813-15
Written by Himself
Edited by John H. Lewis

ILLUSTRATED

FIRST EDITION IN THIS FORM

First published within four volumes broadly under the title
'Reminiscences of Captain R. H. Gronow'

Leonaur is an imprint of Oakpast Ltd

Copyright in this form © 2023 Oakpast Ltd

ISBN: 978-1-916535-46-6 (hardcover)
ISBN: 978-1-916535-47-3 (softcover)

http://www.leonaur.com

Publisher's Notes

The views expressed in this book are not necessarily
those of the publisher.

Contents

Sir Arthur Wellesley, 1st Duke of Wellington

DEDICATION

This book is dedicated to the memory of the late, Ian Robertson (1928-2021), Hispanophile and one of our finest historians of the Peninsular War. His kindness and encouragement will never be forgotten.

First Foot Guards in winter kit

Introduction to this Edition by the Editor

The reason this comparatively small book came into being is a simple one. I knew of 'Captain Gronow's Reminiscences' for decades before I ever wrote or edited military history, because we had at home a comparatively modern edition of them which was comprised of selections from the four original editions that broadly embraced that title. So, of course, I knew he had once been an officer of the First Guards in his younger days, because several of the anecdotes in this book of ours concerned that period of his life. Most of Gronow's reminiscences were not of a military nature—it is fair to say—being concerned with personalities of note and society gossip of the Regency period and thereafter, as most people familiar with them know.

The years rolled by and, without going into details this introduction or the reader does not need to make its point, I then found myself as a publisher of military history books. That occupation brought me, in due course, to the creating of a book concerning the military career of Lord Saltoun, which I titled, 'The March to Hougoumont'.

As one might expect in researching material for that book, I required the confirmatory and supporting accounts of other soldiers of Saltoun's regiment, the First Foot Guards (or as they became after the Battle of Waterloo in 1815), the Grenadier Guards. The fact is, however, that compared to certain other regiments of the British Army of that period, The Grenadier Guards did not have so many authors of useful information upon which one could draw. Among those that I could discover, Gronow's anecdotes were distinctive, because the style in which his observations were delivered was companionable, intimately detailed, entertaining, occasionally amusing and Saltoun actually appeared within them.

All that having been said, the modern reader could only regret that, when it came to his military memories, Gronow had not been as forthcoming as he was about the intimacies of the high society of his time which—to be fair—though invaluable in creating a flavour of the period, have not weathered the intervening years quite as well as his military writings have done. Fame is a fleet-footed entity and most of the society celebrities of Gronow's time had predictably short spans in the popular memory, just as those from later times have or will henceforth. His eyewitness testament concerning great events on the stage of history, by contrast, is a precious repository of source material. Ironically Gronow makes apologies for his writings on the Battle of Waterloo among so many other writers—from his perspective—who he felt had overworked the subject. Had he but known the truth of the matter viewed from a century and a half in the future, especially so far as the Grenadier Guards were concerned!

Whilst we are fortunate to have Gronow's invaluable military observations, until the publication of this edition—so far as I am aware—they have never been collected together in a dedicated single volume and equally have never been arranged in chronological order—scattered as they originally were throughout his four (three more correctly) books. That situation seemed a shame to me that required rectification, because hitherto Gronow's martial recollections would not necessarily readily find their way into the hands and libraries of those most specifically interested in reading them. So, if a remedy was genuinely required for that shortcoming—here it is!

Need it be emphasised I cannot claim very much authorship regarding this endeavour since (before the age of the personal computer) anyone with a modicum of knowledge of the subject could have assembled its contents with the aid of a pair of scissors and a pot of paste. That having be admitted, apparently no one has thus far thought to do it, though it is worth noting that individual anecdotes have been required to be disassembled and reassembled with other constituent parts to reveal a consistently flowing narrative. Fortunately, most of Gronow's anecdotes fall readily into that framework, but inevitably—when the task was completed—I found I had some left over that did not seem to naturally fit anywhere within the principal text. So, I have included them for readers interest in the 'miscellany' that forms the final part of this book.

As I have pointed out, Gronow's anecdotes of the latter stages of the Peninsular War and Campaign of 1815 remain fewer than we might wish and so, partly for that reason, require a certain amount of wider historical knowledge covering the period after the fall of San Sebastian in 1813 to the battles of Quatre Bras, Waterloo and the march and occupation of Paris and thereafter in 1815, to give them context.

So, to assist in that respect I have once again (since I had visited it frequently and employed it extensively for the creation of, 'The March to Hougoumont'), drawn upon Hamilton's 'History of the Grenadier Guards'. I have employed those elements of the history of the regiment that correspond with Gronow's service and glimpses of wider events that appear within it to link Gronow's words in their proper place. Written in the middle years of the 19th century, Hamilton's work was predictably written in a flowery style of his day, so I have modestly edited it to make the elements I have employed more readable for contemporary consumption. I have also excised certain passages that did not particularly contribute to Gronow's narrative—more metaphorical cutting and pasting, in fact.

As a word of caution, the same cannot be said for the introduction that follows this one, because it came from an edition published shortly after Gronow's death and so is written in the to be expected archaic style. It has been edited by me to eradicate some of its worse irrelevant excesses and so legitimately provides interesting background concerning the man and his original project.

It would be wrong to withhold from the reader that, peculiarly, whilst the young ensigns with whom Gronow sailed to Spain appear regularly in the Hamilton history, Gronow's name—particularly in the early period—remains markedly absent. There could be several explanations for this since Hamilton's work has not proven to be infallibly accurate on other matters in including impartiality or inclusivity. I have not, on this occasion, corrected Hamilton's assertions where later scholarship has been at odds with them, since that was never the purpose of this book. It is therefore best viewed as entirely a period piece in that regard.

I assume that most—if not all—the readers of this kind of book have some knowledge of the events that led to young Rees Gronow stepping ashore in Spain in 1813, but in the event some background is required, it now follows in the fewest number of words I can manage to explain it. Any reader who does not need such an explanation should skip the following three paragraphs.

The French Revolution spread its philosophical ideals across Europe but emphasised them by means of a motivated and successful army. Spain became an ally fighting with the French at Trafalgar, but Napoleon ere long decided that he would prefer to see both Portugal and Spain within his expanding First Empire of the French.

The French invaded in 1807 usurping the Spanish throne and placing Joseph Bonaparte upon it. The Iberian nations resisted aided by a British Army which was initially victorious in Portugal in 1808 under the generalship of the man who would become the Duke of Wellington, but who was thereafter recalled to bear his portion of a shortcoming demonstrably not his fault. His place was taken by Sir John Moore whose expedition did not fare well and whose army had to be evacuated. Moore was killed in the final battle at Corunna in 1809. The exonerated 'Wellington' replaced him and fought the French together with Portuguese and Spanish Allies with varying degrees of success, but never suffering outright defeat. Eventually the tide of war turned in the Allies' favour in all theatres of the war following the debacle of Napoleon's invasion of Russia and the French in Spain were pushed back towards their own frontiers defined by the Pyrenees Mountains.

Wellington's forces delivered a crushing defeat in the north of Spain at Vittoria and other French defeats in the north and east of Europe meant that the die was cast for Napoleon's fall. He would not however go down without a fight and the final battles in the south would take place in 1813 on the soil of France itself.

Finally, readers are encouraged not to take Gronow's recording of corps or regiments in the French Army entirely literally. He was not an expert, never offered himself as an historian and is best considered as a writer of impressions rather than indelible facts. Likewise, his claim to have witnessed a killing shot with a 'Brown Bess' musket at 400 yards is perhaps—taken literally—more possible than probable, so readers should content themselves with the knowledge that (specifics aside) this was 'a very fine or exceedingly fortunate shot at a very long range'. None of these shortcomings, I venture to suggest, take anything away from Gronow's contribution to the intimate history of the pivotal events he witnessed.

JHL, 2023

Privates of the First Foot Guards on service

Concerning Captain Gronow and His Recollections Edited from an Original Introduction

After detailing his store of anecdotes to his contemporaries for a couple of generations, Captain Gronow was induced to take up his pen, and commit to print an experimental instalment of the incidents with which he had hitherto regaled his friends *vivâ voce*, with light rapid touch, and in a brisk unaffected style which preserves the point of lively converse.

Captain Gronow modestly observes his *Reminiscences* are merely fragmental and miniature illustrations of contemporary history, and, in the eyes of posterity, it is this circumstance which gives value to his anecdotes; the subjects recorded by his pen are, of necessity, for the most part outside the province of graver historians or more serious biographers, and are precisely those familiar sketches which fill in realistic details, and supply the essentials of local colour.

The first series appeared in 1862, and met with a flattering reception. The writer, as he averred, was able to recall, with all their original vividness, scenes which occurred in his early days, nature having endowed him with the retentive faculty of "distinctly recollecting the face, walk, and voice, as well as the dress and general manner of every one whom he had known."

It had been the lot of Captain Gronow, as he informed his readers: "To have lived through the greater part of one of the most eventful centuries of England's history; to be thrown amongst most of the remarkable men of his day, whether soldiers, statesmen, men of letters, theatrical people, or those whose birth and fortune—rather, perhaps, than their virtues and talents—have caused them to be conspicuous at home and abroad."

The writer, from motives of delicacy, omitted much which, though lively and interesting even beyond what he has left us, he thought it expedient to withhold from publication, no less from respect to the memory of the dead, than out of consideration for the sensibilities of the living. In the pictures which hung in the long gallery of his memory, Captain Gronow thought proper to "confine himself to facts and characteristics which were familiar to the circles in which he lived, and perhaps are as much public property as the painted portraits of celebrities." The reviewers pronounced the writer's manner possessed "the merit of a sensible man of the world's freedom from egotism."

Captain Gronow was deferentially apologetic as to possible defects of style, due to inexperience, merely claiming to have jotted down the anecdotes "in the best way he could." He wrote: "Soldiers are not generally famous for literary excellence, and when I was young, the military man was, perhaps, much less a scholar than he is at the present day."

The initial series, *Anecdotes of the Camp, the Court, and the Clubs, at the close of the last war with France*, was indulgently received beyond the expectations of the writer, and Captain Gronow was encouraged to redeem a conditional promise that, if his work met with the approbation of the public, he hoped to publish, from the materials stored in his memory, a further repertory of similar nature. A second series of reminiscences appeared in 1863, particularly dealing with the events of 1815, and that momentous struggle, of which the writer was not only an eye-witness, but also bore the dangers of the day with his comrades of the Guards: "Though the battle of Waterloo is almost a hackneyed subject, yet it has been latterly so frequently brought forward by French writers of celebrity, that I have thought some further observations might not prove altogether without interest."

This paragraph refers more immediately to the works of M. Thiers, Colonel Charras, Quinet's *Defence of Marshal Ney*, and Victor Hugo's romance of *Les Miserables*.

In his brief preface to the Second series of *Recollections and Anecdotes*, Captain Gronow, with excellent taste, begs the indulgence of his readers for the occasional introduction of sentences in foreign idioms, unavoidable under the circumstances, where no English equivalents are available, and the spirit of the original would be sacrificed by a vernacular rendering.

The third series of Captain Gronow's *Recollections*, which appeared in 1865, was devoted to "Celebrities of London and Paris," and, amongst the special features, the writer, as an eye-witness, detailed his experiences of the *Coup d'État*, which, according to his convictions, restored prosperity and power to France; the imperial dynasty had his sympathy, and as he did not live to see the defects of the Third Empire and the sudden downfall of Napoleon III., his reminiscences naturally refer to that sovereign as the ruler of the French nation.

Captain Gronow lived to prepare a fourth and concluding series of *Reminiscences and Anecdotes*, and, while the proofs of the volume were in the hands of the writer for final revision, there came the unexpected news of his death, which occurred in Paris, 20th November, 1865; the work was issued in 1866 as *Captain Gronow's Last Recollections*. As with the premonition of his own approaching end, the author mournfully wrote: "I have lived long enough to have lost all my dearest and best friends. The great laws of humanity have left me on a high and dry elevation, from which I am doomed to look over a sort of Necropolis, whence it is my delight to call forth choice spirits of the past."

The professional career and subsequent life of Captain Gronow are fairly and sufficiently chronicled incidentally in the pages of his personal recollections. "Nothing extenuate nor set down aught in malice," the principle he meted out to others, should justly be his right. He was apparently a favoured child of fortune, was presented with a commission in the Grenadier Guards on leaving Eton—in the stirring days of the Peninsular War the youth of England early received its "baptism of fire,"—and from the age of sixteen, Gronow mixed freely with that select community emphatically described as "the world"—otherwise the favoured portion of society.

He joyfully accepted and with keen enjoyment took his part in fashionable life with characteristic complacency and nonchalance; from early days appreciating to the full all that life could offer to a "dandy guardsman"—the excitement of campaigning, a well-filled purse, social gaiety, congenial associates—"fair women and brave men,"—with, for a season, a seat in the first Reformed Parliament. It may be interesting to note that—to account for certain mysterious but unauthenticated rumours of distinguished and even royal patronage, characteristic of the young guardsman's generation—the family of Captain Gronow claimed royal descent. He was the son of William Gronow of Court Herbert. On the authority of Sir Bernard Burke ("Landed Gentry"), the Gronows were a very ancient family originally seated in North Wales, where they had large landed possessions.

In the reign of Edward III., Sir Tudor ap Gronow, an ancestor of the regal house of Tudor, claimed the honour of knighthood, for by the laws and constitution of King Arthur he deemed himself entitled to that distinction upon the ground of possessing the following threefold qualifications—birth, estate, and valour. King Edward III., being pleased with the bold and lordly mien of Sir Tudor ap Gronow, was induced to confer the honour upon him. Owen Tudor, the grandson of this bold knight, married the widow of Henry V., and their son, Jasper Tudor, Earl of Richmond, was the father of Henry VII. Being thus regally connected, the family scutcheon bears in its quarterings the lions of England. In the choir of St. David's Cathedral there remain two recumbent effigies in armour, representing two members of this family. On the breast and back of each figure is sculptured a lion rampant, that in one of them being differenced by a label.

The writer passed so much of his life in Paris, and has drawn such animated pictures of French society, that it is amusing—as a contrast to his own impressions of Parisian celebrities—to learn the opinions of a foreign contemporary upon Captain Gronow, and this we are enabled to do from the pages of M. H. de Villemessant's *Memoirs of a Journalist*, published in 1872.

Mr. Gronow, when I knew him, was small, spare, and about fifty years of age. His hair was thinning, and he wore a small moustache, of which the edge was daily shaved, which did not disguise the circumstance that the captain's latent vanity had recourse to a brown dye. He always wore a blue tight-fitting coat, closely buttoned, just allowing a narrow line of white waistcoat to be visible.

It was customary, in certain circles, to lay wagers that he slept with the top of his gold-headed cane between his lips. This action was characteristic. With the head of his well-known stick pressed to his lips, the captain spent his days, seated at the window, watching every one he knew in Paris pass the Petit Cercle, of which he was one of the founders, and where the latter part of his life was spent. This Cercle was a small and select club, occupying a suite of rooms in the Café de Paris, on the Boulevard des Italiens.

He was very 'good form,' had a great respect for everything that was proper and convenient, and a strong propensity to become eccentric. He committed the greatest follies, without in the slightest disturbing the points of his shirt collar. He had married a lady of the *corps de ballet*, and would rather have blown out his brains than have gone to the opera in morning costume.

This little man, with his hair well arranged, scented, cold, and phlegmatic, knew the best people in Paris, visited all the diplomats, and was evidently intimate with everybody of note in Europe.

A natural reserve, which prevented Gronow from enlarging, amongst comparative strangers, upon his family connections, led, in the minds of slight acquaintances who had no better information on the subject, to vague and romantic surmises as to his origin; opinion wavered between the assumption that the captain was the descendant of a race of wealthy retired brewers, and the more popular hypothesis, that he was the illegitimate son of an exalted personage. It was rumoured that his mother had been very intimate with Mrs. Jordan, and that it was due to this influence that young Gronow had obtained a company in the Grenadier Guards at the outset of his career. These imaginary antecedents must be dismissed as the fabrications of ignorant gossip; the French writer merely recorded the irresponsible tittle-tattle floating on the surface, and he, moreover, seems to have confused his remembrances of the captain with certain episodes related in Gronow's own *Recollections*; a certain Captain Hesse, a putative son of the Duke of York, was probably the actual hero of the following apocryphal anecdote M. de Villemessant relates:

> Gronow was one of the prettiest dandy officers of proud Albion, and for years his miniature portrait was secretly carried about by a great princess who was madly in love with him, and sometimes, when a fashionable beauty was passing, he was observed carelessly opening the red morocco case in which he found again the souvenirs of his youth and his successes; then he sighed and shut it again. This was the only proof of sensibility he ever gave.

On the same authority, "classical" and "thoroughbred" were the two words with which the subject of these curious revelations expressed his admiration for female beauty. The journalist writes:

> The princess must have spent some very happy moments. Gronow belonged to the school of 'silent diplomatists,' which implies that he said a great deal, and spoke diffusely whenever he made up his mind to unburden himself."
>
> He was fond of English literature, and though he had not much sympathy with the character and politics of Lord Byron, Gronow greatly valued him as a poet. This little man, who had a face like marble, felt very deeply, a contrast not altogether exceptional.
>
> Perhaps he had been obliged to conceal his feelings, the better to baffle prying looks when he was not kneeling at the feet of his princess (still that fair personage of Fairyland!), and he had never been able to throw off the mask. But when he was extolling the sombre and impressive

creations of Byron no one could doubt that passion had formerly dwelt in the heart of this man of past experiences.

With genuine enthusiasm he analysed the tempests which must have raged in the souls of the heroes of his favourite poet, of the Giaour, the *Corsair*, and above all of Lara, whom he claimed to have known; for, if Gronow may be credited, Lara and Manfred really existed, and their living prototype was the once well-known Captain Trelawney, who became very intimate with Lord Byron in Greece. Gronow related certain of Trelawney's adventures without hesitation—sometimes in an impassioned tone of voice, but (according to habit) without ever ceasing to rub his chin with the handle of his stick. And when his auditors inquired 'What subsequently became of this hero of romance?' he replied: 'I don't know. Trelawney now eats pudding in England, and does not care for us!'

Mention has been made above of his marriage with Mlle. Didier of the Paris Opera, but it remains to be said that Captain Gronow espoused in a second marriage Mlle, de St. Pol, a lady belonging to an old and noble family of Brittany. Four children were born of the marriage, two of whom are still living. The second Madame Gronow, who still survives, (1900), was the constant adviser and devoted companion of her husband during the last years of his life, and it is interesting to learn that while Captain Gronow's latter years were occupied in recording these reminiscences, they were cheered by the society of his wife and family.

The Later Peninsular War Campaign in the South of France

Before describing the march of the First Guards through the north of Spain in the summer of 1813, it is necessary to describe briefly to the progress of the Allied Army under Wellington, before whom the French were at this time retiring to the frontiers of France.

The British general had determined in May to operate upon the French right, by marching through Tras os Montes in the north of Portugal. For this purpose, a corps of five divisions, 40,000 men, under Lieutenant-General Graham, forming the left wing of the army, crossed the Douro and reached Braganza on the 22nd of that month. Wellington then advanced with his own corps of 30,000 on Alba and Salamanca; turning northward towards Zanura, and the two armies united at Carcagales on the 30th and 31st. The Spanish troops under General Freyre, also effected a junction, the Allied Army in the field on the right bank of the Douro amounted to 90,000 men and 100 guns, and on the 4th of June Wellington commenced his march towards the frontiers of France.

Napoleon's brother, the usurper King of Spain, Joseph was at Valladolid with 52,000 men and 100 guns, but the strategical position of the British general enabled him, by continually pushing forward his left, to compel the French to abandon every position in succession. Wellington was at the Carrion on the 7th, and on the 12th of June in sight of Burgos. The enemy blew up the castle and retired, anxious to put the defile of Parnorbo between himself and the Allies, but Graham acting on the left, and

First Foot Guards in Spain

marching by a route hitherto regarded as impracticable, crossed the Ebro at Frias on the 15th, and getting into the rear of the French right, cut them off from the coast. Wellington was thus enabled to establish for himself a new base of operations on the sea, and the British fleet entered Santander—creating a port of supply.

It was at this time that orders were sent to Oporto in Portugal for the First Brigade of Guards to move up to the front. Graham still pushed on, driving back Reille's corps of 8,000 men at Osma to Anana, and on the evening of the 20th he halted at Marguia. Wellington won the decisive Battle of Vittoria on the 21st of June, initiating a total rout of the French Army, 151 guns were captured on the field, and stores of all kinds fell into the hands of the victors. The French general, Foy, retreated, pursued by Graham; and after garrisoning San Sebastian, crossed the Bidassoa into France. Graham invested San Sebastian on the 9th of July, and on the 24th made an attempt to storm it: the assault, however, was repulsed with heavy loss.

Soult had recently arrived from Germany to take command of the French Army, and having reorganised his forces, advanced to turn the British right, and relieve Pampeluna, upon which Wellington converted the siege of San Sebastian into a blockade, met the French, and, after a series of combats which lasted from the 25th to the 30th of July, carried the position in front of Sorauren, forcing the enemy to retreat, and on the 2nd of August the French were driven across the frontier, permanently abandoning the Spanish Peninsula.

The siege of San Sebastian was renewed, but fire was not opened until the 26th August, before which time the First Brigade of Guards, whose march from Oporto will now be recorded, arrived on the scene of action, and on the 18th of August marched into camp, joining the First Division.

Leaving Lieutenant-Colonel Tinling at Oporto in charge of the sick, the regiment, under the brigade-command of Major-General Lambert, commenced its march from Oporto on the 29th of June. On the 11th of August it passed by the Puerto de

Francia, where all the artillery captured in the Battle of Vittoria and during the retreat, amounting to 210 guns was parked. On the 18th of the same month the First Guards marched into camp at Oyarzun, two miles from Irun, and joined their comrades of the Second Brigade. On the 28th of August they advanced still nearer to Irun, where they acted as a covering force to the troops of the Fifth Division, who were engaged in the siege of San Sebastian.

The camp was well situated, about one mile from Irun, in an old wood upon the face of the mountain, from where the Bidassoa, the French lines, St. Jean de Luz, and Bayonne in the distance, were visible. The Second Brigade was encamped on the left of the First, and further still the Germans. The Bidassoa, from low water to half-tide, was fordable, but the ground in front of the Guards camp was very strong, and there was not much likelihood of the enemy attacking that side of the position. Major-General Lambert resigned his command on being appointed to a brigade in the sixth division. Colonel Peregrine Maitland succeeded to the First Guards Brigade, and Lieutenant-Colonel Stuart to the Third Battalion.

The left wing of the Allied Army, under Graham, was now composed of the First Division under Major-General Howard; the Fifth Division under Major-General Leith; Lord Aylmer's brigade; and a Spanish Army under Freyre. The Fifth Division, consisting of Major-Generals Hay's and Robinson's brigades, was employed in carrying on the operations of the siege of San Sebastian; the First Division formed the covering force and guarded the line of the Bidassoa from the Crown Mountain to the left, while Freyre's Spanish corps was posted to the right, on the heights of San Marcial. The order of battle of the First Division was thus constituted. The First Guards on the right, Hinuber's Germans on their left, then Stopford's Second Brigade of Guards, and the German light infantry on the extreme left.

By the 30th of August the enemy's guns on the ramparts of San Sebastian were silenced, and the walls breached in two places so the assault was to take place on the following morn-

THE STORMING OF SAN SEBASTIAN

ing. Wellington had objected to opinions expressed by officers of the Fifth Division regarding the practicability of storming the breach, since the failure on the 24th of July, and thought that the men of that division would be discouraged. So, he ordered 400 men of the First Division—200 of the division of Guards and 200 of the King's German Legion—and 350 of the Fourth and Light Divisions "to show the way to the breach if it should be practicable." The storming party of the Guards, consisting of 100 men of the first and 100 men from the Second Brigade, under the command of Lieutenant-Colonel Cooke of the First Guards, marched at 6 p.m. from camp, with the other detachments from the division, and encamped about two miles from the fortress. They moved off again about two in the morning of the 31st, and occupied the ruined convent of St. Bartolomeo, where they remained until half-past nine.

Leith commanded the assaulting columns, and would not allow the volunteers to lead the way, but placed them in support to Robinson's brigade. The troops were exposed to a heavy fire on their way to the breach, the appearance of which was misleading, as it could not be entered except in single file. They attacked in succession, tried to effect a foothold, but were struck down by their hundreds. The volunteers demanded "why they had been brought there if they were not to lead the assault?" and at last, let loose, they went like a whirlwind to the breach and swarmed up the ruins. Many were killed on the crest, and, though repeated attempts were made, only the dead or wounded remained on the summit.

At last Graham ordered the artillery to open over the heads of the stormers to clear the ramparts. By sheer chance a shell ignited a store of powder and combustibles, which the enemy had prepared to spring in the event of the ramparts being gained. The explosions were enormous and, during the ensuing chaos, the stormers forced their way forwards and entered the town. The governor withdrew to the citadel, and, on the 9th of September, surrendered.

The losses of the division of Guards on this occasion were as usual severe. Casualties among the officers of the First Guards were one officer, Ensign Burrard, of the first battalion (a son of Sir Harry Burrard), mortally wounded and one officer, Ensign Orlando Bridgeman, wounded. There were, in round numbers, 150 casualties amongst the 200 Guardsmen involved. The total losses were 1500 men.

Soult made one more attempt to relieve the fortress on the morning of the assault, by threatening the allied left: but it was easily repulsed. During this attempt the First Division was drawn up in support, in rear of Irun, but was not engaged. The enemy withdrew within their own frontier on the same day.

As the British Army prepared to enter France, in Germany, the French emperor fought at bay which had considerable influence upon the war on the Spanish frontiers. After the disastrous retreat of the French from Russia, Prussia had joined the Russian alliance, and Austria was preparing to fight. Napoleon, however, rapidly collected another army of 200,000 men and 350 guns, with which, in May, he fought and won the battles of Lützen and Bautzen. Austria on the 27th of August, was defeated with heavy loss at Dresden.

From that time Napoleon's good fortunes irredeemably declined. The Allies, 250,000 strong, again opposed him at Leipzig, and after three days' combat, gained a decisive victory, which eventually obliged the emperor to retire across the Rhine, and the Allies in pursuit subsequently entered France at different points.

At the other end of the scale of great events, the young Rees Gronow, aged 19 years, was preparing to make his entrance onto their stage as a warrior:—

★★

After leaving Eton, I received an ensign's commission in the First Guards during the month of December, 1812. Though many years have elapsed, I still remember my boyish delight at being named to so distinguished a regiment, and at the prospect of soon taking a part in the glorious deeds of our army in

Spain. I joined in February, 1813, and cannot but recollect with astonishment how limited and imperfect was the instruction which an officer received at that time; he absolutely entered the army without any military education whatever.

We were so defective in our drill, even after we had passed out of the hands of the sergeant, that the excellence of our non-commissioned officers alone prevented us from meeting with the most fatal disasters in the face of the enemy. Physical force and our bulldog energy carried many a hard-fought field.

Luckily, *nous avons changé tout cela*, and our officers may now vie with those of any other army in an age when the great improvements in musketry, in artillery practice, and in the greater rapidity of manoeuvring, have entirely changed the art of war, and rendered the individual education of those in every grade of command an absolute necessity.

After passing through the hands of the drill sergeant with my friends Dashwood, Batty, Browne, Lascelles, Hume, and Master, and mounting guard at St. James's for a few months, we were hurried off, one fine morning, in charge of a splendid detachment of five hundred men to join Lord Wellington in Spain.

Macadam had just begun to do for England what Marshal Wade did in Scotland seventy years before; and we were able to march twenty miles a day with ease until we reached Portsmouth. There we found transports ready to convey a large reinforcement, of which we formed part, to Lord Wellington, who was now making his arrangements, after taking St. Sebastian, for a yet more important event in the history of the Peninsular War—the invasion of France.

We sailed under convoy of the *Madagascar* frigate, commanded by Captain Curtis; and, after a favourable voyage, we arrived at Passages. Our stay there was short, for we were ordered to join the army without loss of time. In three hours, we got fairly into camp, where we were received with loud cheers by our brothers in arms. The whole British Army was here under canvas; our Allies, the Spaniards and Portuguese, being in the rear.

There was a wide difference in the camp life of the English and French Armies. An English soldier in camp appeared to be the most uncomfortable of mortals; there was no plan laid down for his recreation, or the employment of his leisure hours, and you might see him either brushing his clothes or cleaning his accoutrements, or else sitting on his knapsack, smoking his pipe to pass the time. We had no large tent wherein the men could congregate to converse, read, or otherwise amuse themselves, and when the weather was wet, they huddled together in small tents, where the atmosphere was worse than that of the Black Hole of Calcutta. The pipe-clay system of tormenting our men, by requiring them to keep their kits clean, and punishing them by extra drills if the firelock or belts were not as spotless as on parade at the Horse Guards, was (to say the least of it) extremely injudicious.

The French soldiers, on the other hand, had small tents, amply large enough for five or six men, or, in default of these, they constructed tents with earth, trees, and rushes. Streets were formed, with squares; places of amusement were planned, and large trenches were dug in every direction, to drain the ground thoroughly. The officers, if near a town, took possession of the best lodgings, for the convenience of coffee-houses and kitchens; but, although they had every luxury they could afford or procure, their motto was, "*À la guerre comme la guerre.*"On entering a French camp, you saw as much order as in the best regulated towns. *Gendarmes* kept strict watch over the soldiers, a fire-brigade was always in readiness, and everything was arranged methodically. A *cantinière* was attached to the camp, and supplied the officers and men with wine and spirits according to regulations.

Early in the year 1812 the Duke of York had despatched to the seat of war the 3rd Battalion of my old regiment. It was considered by military men to have been the finest in his Majesty's service. All the men, with the exception of the grenadier company, were strong, active young fellows, but had not seen active service. They were conveyed to Cadiz in men-of-war, and arrived there without any accident; but owing to change of diet, and the substituting the horrid wine of the country for the porter they had been accustomed to at home, before the expiration of a few weeks, five hundred of these fine fellows died in the hospital at Vizu, and were buried in the churchyard there. I mention this to show how careful commanding officers ought to be to prevent similar consequences from decimating bodies of fresh troops: although warnings of this sort have occurred all over the globe.

On joining my regiment in the Peninsula, one of the grenadiers, a tall and well-built man, was recommended to me as the best person to employ for pitching my tent. This man had been brought up as a carpenter, but through some misunderstanding with his relations had enlisted. While cutting the trench he entered into conversation with me, and said he hoped, as I appeared very young and unaccustomed to bivouacking, that I would forgive him for being so bold as to offer a little salutary advice: which was, to drink every morning on rising a small glass of brandy or rum, as by so doing rheumatism, dysentery, and many other camp disorders, would be prevented. He added, with tears in his eyes, that he had lost his brother at Vizu, owing to his not following the advice he was now giving me. I was so struck with the earnest manner of the man that I adopted his panacea, and during the whole time that I was in camp I never had a day's illness.

★★★

Wellington remained inactive for a month after the fall of San Sebastian, waiting for the policy of the Allies in Germany to be ratified, because they had not at that time decided upon an invasion of France. He was reluctant to advance before he could depend upon a diversion on its eastern frontier which would be to his strategic benefit. Urged, however, by the British government to provide the diversion in the south himself to assist the continental sovereigns, who were then preparing for the final blow against the French emperor at Leipzig, he made his plans for the advance.

★★

I knew an officer of the 18th Hussars, W. R., young, rich, and a fine-looking fellow, who joined the army not far from St. Sebastian. His stud of horses was remarkable for their blood; his grooms were English, and three in number. He brought with him a light cart to carry forage, and a *fourgon* for his own baggage. All went on well till he came to go on outpost duty; but not finding there any of the comforts to which he had been accustomed, he quietly mounted his charger, told his astonished sergeant that campaigning was not intended for a gentleman, and instantly galloped off to his quarters, ordering his servants to pack up everything immediately, as he had hired a transport to take him off to England. He left us before anyone had time to stop him; and though despatches were sent off to the commander-in-chief, requesting that a court martial might sit to try the young deserter, he arrived home long enough before the despatches to enable him to sell out of his regiment. He deserved to have been shot.

★★

Wellington commenced operations early in October, by forcing the passage of the Bidassoa, and treading, for the first time, upon the soil of Southern France. A considerable range of mountains rose opposite the allied position, separating the valleys of the Bidassoa and the Nivelle Rivers. Wellington's plan was to seize, with his right and centre, the highest point of these mountains, La Rhune, and its dependent ridges, while on his extreme left, he would obtain possession of Fuenterabia. The French position to the north of the Bidassoa was already very strong, and Soult had strengthened it with additional works. He anticipated that the allied Anglo-Spanish Army would attack his centre and left, and he was unprepared for the bold movement which Wellington executed of passing the Bidassoa at its mouth

ON THE MARCH IN SPAIN

PENINSULAR ARMY IN CAMP

at low water, where the tide rises sixteen feet, and the sands are half a mile across. The First Division of Guards and the Fifth Division, together with some foreign troops, forming the left wing of the Allied Army, were nominated carry out this part of the attack.

Upon the left wing were, the two brigades of Guards and Brigadier-General Wilson's Portuguese brigade would pass the Bidassoa, by the ford, at a ruined bridge, and by two fords a little lower down the river, the lower one of which is called the Vado de las Nasas de Abaxo, and is near the point where the *chaussée* from Irun first comes upon the. banks of the river. Some of these battalions were to pass at a ford a short distance above the ruined bridge, and all were to begin their advance upon the fords at the same time that the Fifth Division from Fuenterabia began to move forward. They were to assemble before dawn, near Irun, concealed until the moment of attack and then move forward simultaneously to the various fords.

A rocket from the steeple of Fuenterabia would be the signal for the advance of the brigades of Guards, as soon as the Fifth Division was ready to move, and because the river bends to the right below the bridge of Irun, it was necessary that the division on the extreme left should slightly precede the rest of the attack. Part of the 12th Light Dragoons, with the brigade of artillery attached to the First Division, and a brigade of reserve artillery, were to pass over with these columns, while other guns were to cover the passage from the most available heights of San Marcial, Lord Alymer's brigade forming the reserve to the first division, behind the slopes of that mountain.

The first objective of the Guards after crossing was to establish themselves upon the opposite hill called Montaine de Louis XIV., and on other advantageous points, keeping up a communication on their left, if possible, with the Fifth Division. The troops were all to be in position at seven o'clock in the morning, low water being expected at a quarter past. The passage of the Bidassoa had to be accomplished with precision and resolution because the troops that had crossed the river would be prevented from returning for several hours by the rising tide.

★★★

About the middle of October, to our great delight, the army received orders to cross the Bidassoa. At three o'clock on the morning of the 15th our regiment advanced through a difficult country, and, after a harassing march, reached the top of a hill as the grey light of morning began to dawn. We marched in profound silence, but with a pleasurable feeling of excitement amongst all ranks at the thought of meeting the enemy, and perhaps with not an equally agreeable idea that we might be in the next world before the day was over.

As we ascended the rugged side of the hill, I saw, for the first time, the immortal Wellington. He was very stern and grave-looking; he was in deep meditation, so long as I kept him in view, and spoke to no one. His features were bold, and I saw much decision of character in his expression. He rode a knowing-looking, thoroughbred horse, and wore a grey overcoat, Hessian boots, and a large cocked hat.

He was accompanied by the Spanish general, Alava, Lord Fitzroy Somerset, and Major, afterward Colonel Freemantle, about whom we heard an interesting anecdote. When the British Army was in full retreat from Burgos, Freemantle was sent by Lord Wellington to look out for comfortable quarters for himself and his staff. Freemantle, after galloping over many miles of desolate country, could only discover a hut.

Accordingly, a good fire was prepared for the commander of the forces, and every preparation made for his reception. After Freemantle had communicated with His Lordship, he lost no time in returning, when, to his surprise, he found the hut occupied by an officer of the line, who, standing with his back turned to the blazing fire, was whistling "for want of thought." The *aide-de-camp* politely told the officer that the hut had been secured for Lord Wellington, and therefore begged he would retire. The officer flatly refused, saying he would not give it up to Lord Wellington, or to Old Nick himself. "Well,

PASSAGE OF THE BIDASSOA

then, I must use force: the provost-marshal shall be sent for, whose prisoner you will be until a court martial shall sit for disobedience of orders." The officer surrendered at discretion, and was never more seen at headquarters.

This anecdote was told to Beau Brummell at White's Club by Freemantle on his return to England, whereupon the beau exclaimed: "If I had been in your place, Freemantle, I should have rung the bell, and desired the servants to kick the fellow downstairs,"

★★★

At three o'clock in the morning of the 7th of October the First Division was under arms, and, leaving its tents standing, passed through Irun, and arrived at the rendezvous at the appointed time, without having been observed by the enemy, in which they were assisted by a violent thunderstorm, which burst over the French position. Upon the signal, the advance of the First Division was made; not a shot had yet been fired; the several fords were approached, and the French were completely taken by surprise.

Under cover of a heavy fire of artillery from the heights of San Marcial, the right column of the First Division, principally Wilson's Portuguese, supported by the two battalions of First Guards, crossed the river in front of the lower heights of San Marcial, taking the higher right hand fords, and advanced upon the enemy. The left column, or Second Brigade of Guards, preceded by the German light infantry, crossed the river at the ford, near the broken bridge, and formed on the right of the Fifth Division, covering the formation of a pontoon bridge for the passage of artillery. The right column of the Fifth Division, after crossing the river, drove the French from the village of Andaya on the right bank, and continued to advance rapidly on Croix de Bouquet.

★★★

We commenced the passage of the Bidassoa about five in

the morning, and in a short time infantry, cavalry, and artillery found themselves upon French ground. The stream at the point we forded was nearly four feet deep, and had Soult been aware of what we were about, we should have found the passage of the river a very arduous undertaking.

Three miles above, we discovered the French Army, and ere long found ourselves under fire. The sensation of being made a target to a large body of men is at first not particularly pleasant, but, "in a trice, the ear becomes more Irish, and less nice." The first man I ever saw killed was a Spanish soldier, who was cut in two by a cannonball.

★★

The French, opposed to the First Brigade, under Maitland, did not await the close approach of the British Guards, but retired, leaving three guns in their hands; and the left column of the First Division drove the enemy from the Café Republicain, and from the Louis XIV. mountain, also upon Croix de Bouquet, which was the key of the position. After a severe struggle, in which the 9th Regiment met with considerable opposition, the heights were won, and the enemy, being outflanked by the left column of the Fifth Division, gave way; the First Brigade of Guards, continuing its advance, encamped for the night on the heights they had gained, to the right of the high road leading to Urrugne.

★★

The French Army, not long after we began to return their fire, was in full retreat; and after a little sharp, but desultory fighting, in which our division met with some loss, we took possession of the camp and strong position of Soult's army. We found the soldiers' huts very comfortable; they were built of branches of trees and furze, and formed squares and streets, which had names placarded up, such as Rue de Paris, Rue de Versailles, etc. We were not sorry to find ourselves in such commodious quarters, as well as being well housed.

The Guards crossing the Bidassoa

The scenery surrounding the camp was picturesque and grand. From our elevated position, immediately in front, we commanded a wide and extensive plain, intersected by two important rivers, the Nive and the Nivelle. On the right, the lofty Pyrenees, with their grand and varied outline, stood forth conspicuously in a blue, cloudless sky; on our left was the Bay of Biscay, with our cruisers perpetually on the move.

We witnessed from the camp, one night about twelve o'clock, a fight at sea, between an English brig and a French corvette, which was leaving the Adour with provisions and ammunition. She was chased by the brig, and brought to action. The night was sufficiently clear to enable us to discover distinctly the position of the vessels and the measured flash of their guns. They were at close quarters; and in less than half an hour we discovered the crew of the corvette taking to their boats. Shortly afterwards the vessel blew up, with a loud explosion. We came to the conclusion that sea-fighting was more agreeable than land-fighting, as the crews of the vessels engaged without previous heavy marching, and with loose light clothing; there was no manoeuvring, or standing for hours on the defensive; the wounded were immediately taken below and attended to; and the whole affair was over in a pleasingly brief period.

★★★

During the advance of the Light Infantry of the First Guards, under Lord Saltoun, some French wounded were passed, lying by the road side. Lord Saltoun observed one of his men go up to one, and after a moment, put his bayonet through him. He immediately rushed at him, enquiring what he was doing to the wounded Frenchman.

"It's no Frenchman, sir," was the reply; "it's that Evans who deserted the night before the Battle of Corunna." The man was sent to the field hospital, but died the next day. The accusation was correct, he had deserted in January, 1809, had taken service with the French at the commencement of the war, and now, towards its close, in 1818, met his death from the hands of his former comrades, by whom he would not have been recognised, had he not, on seeing the uniform of his old regiment, called out to them for a drink of water.

The fighting had been more severe on the right of the British line, though the French there were also taken by surprise. The Light Division and Giron's Spaniards assaulted the ridge called Bayonette, held by Taupin's division, and, after a severe contest, carried all before them, in spite of the height of the mountain and strength of the works. Freyre's Spaniards had, in the meantime, took the heights before them and, by advancing on St. Jean de Luz, by Joliment, cut off Taupin's line of retreat. The French had succeeded in repelling the attacks made upon the great Rhune Mountain; but Wellington nevertheless forced the French, under Clausel, to abandon it on the following day. The British Army was now in complete possession of the formidable position occupied the day before by the enemy, who retired, and took up a new position for the defence of the line of the Nivelle.

Sir Thomas Graham's health had been failing for some time so he resigned the command of the left wing the day after the passage of the Bidassoa, and was succeeded by Lieutenant-General Sir John Hope. In consequence of the proximity of the armies, there was much outpost duty for the light infantry companies of the Guards, and the advanced sentries of the opposing armies often stood at night within thirty yards of each other.

★★★

The French infantry soldier averaged about five feet five or six in height; in build they were much about what they are now, perhaps a little broader over the shoulder. They were smart, active, handy fellows, and much more able to look after their personal comforts than British soldiers, as their camps indicated. The uniform of those days consisted in a shako, which spread out at the top; a short-waisted, swallow-tailed coat; and large, baggy trousers and gaiters. The clothing of the French soldier was roomy, and enabled him to march and move about at ease: no pipeclay accessories occupied their attention; in a word, their uniforms and accoutrements were infinitely superior to our own, taking into consideration the practical necessities of warfare. The dress of the French soldier was not only loose and comfortable, but easily cleaned, and his knapsack was remarkable for its convenience. Their muskets were inferior to ours, and their firing less deadly. The French cavalry we thought badly horsed; but their uniforms, though showy, were, like those of the infantry, comfortably large and roomy. The French soldier marched quicker than the English, both in advance and retreat, and after a victory by our troops few prisoners were taken. The Duke of Wellington, with all his wonderful foresight and genius, could never get at the secret why so few stragglers were met with in following the enemy; whereas at Burgos, after our raising the siege of that town, indescribable confusion arose, and nearly half the English Army were either left behind or taken prisoners by Soult and Clauzel.

The system of outposts in the French Army was also on a different footing from ours. Before the enemy, the French sentinel was relieved every hour; whereas our soldiers remained on duty two hours!—the extra hour caused great fatigue, and in cold weather induced sleep. A troop of the 11th Light Dragoons on duty in front—that is, at the extreme vedette, in the immediate presence of the enemy—was once caught napping. The French officer in command, observing the bad guard kept, ordered forward a sergeant and five men, who entered our lines and found Captain Wood and his men fast asleep; when the dragoons awoke, they were compelled to surrender themselves prisoners of war.

Now, if the vedette had been changed every hour, this disgraceful catastrophe would not have occurred.

★★

So long as the town of Pampeluna remained in the hands of the French, Wellington had hesitated to advance further; but after a blockade of four months, that town surrendered on the 31st of October, and the British general was now in a position to carry the war into the enemy's country. The French position extended from the seaport of St. Jean de Luz, on their right, nearly due east for about twelve miles, to the hills in front of Souraide and Espelette, and every available point was strengthened by earthworks. The left of the French first line rested on the Nivelle, extending to the right of the Choupara and Mandarin mountains, while Claudet's corps occupied the heights of Ascain and Arnots, between which were the camp of Sare and several strong redoubts.

Since the passage of the Bidassoa, Wellington had observed that Soult had been careful to secure his right flank in front of St. Jean de Luz on the Nivelle, by a triple line of works, that rendered it impregnable; he therefore decided to make only a feigned attack, with his left wing, now under Sir John Hope, on that part of the enemy's line, while he forced the enemy's left, and threatened the rear of his right, so compelling him to withdraw from the strongly-entrenched position in front of St. Jean de Luz.

The previous instructions to Sir John Hope to regulate the attack of the left wing of the army were—He was to operate in three columns. The left column, composed of Halkett's German light infantry, was to act between the heights of Urrugne and the sea coast, fronting northwards towards Socoa Fort; the centre column, or Fifth Division, and some other troops were to occupy the most advantageous points upon the left bank of the rivulet, which runs between the heights of Urrugne and those of Siboure, and when halted were to face towards Siboure and St. Jean de Luz, while the right column, composed of the two brigades of Guards, were to threaten the front of the encampment, which the enemy occupied, on the right bank of the rivulet of Urrugne, and on the British right of the high road leading from that village to St. Jean de Luz, keeping up at the same time the communication on their right with Freyre's Spaniards, who were to attack Ascain. Sir John was particularly instructed that

Map of the
SPANISH CAMPAIGN.

English Miles

0 20 40 60 80 100   200

operations in that quarter were feints and should not be pushed forward as a real attack.

The First Division was still under the command of Major-General Howard, while the First Brigade of Guards was commanded by Major-General Maitland.

The weather had now become wet, which delayed the attack; but, on the morning of the 10th of November the weather improved. During the previous night 100,000 men, with nearly 100 guns, were moved into positions, previously arranged, with so much secrecy, that again the enemy was unaware of the vicinity of so many troops awaiting, in silence, for the signal for battle.

About three o'clock on the morning of the 10th of November, the First and Fifth Divisions descended from the heights on which they had been encamped, and advanced to the line of outposts, arriving an hour before dawn. The French picquets, forming the advanced posts of Reille's and Villatte's divisions, were strongly entrenched, and a large redoubt defended the rising ground in front of Urrugne.

At the given signal of three guns being fired from the Alchabia mountain, 100 guns opened upon the French position, and the army advanced to the attack. On the left, Halkett's German light infantry moved round the hill, whilst the picquets of the First Division, under Lieutenant-Colonel West of the First Guards, made a brisk attack in front, driving the enemy from his advanced position down the hill to the verge of his entrenchments.

The brigades to the left of the First Division moved direct upon Urrugne, while Maitland's Brigade of Guards and Hinuber's Germans advanced against the heights behind Urrugne, which extend towards Ascain. A continued fire was kept up by the light infantry of the First Guards and Germans, but they, of course, received no orders to storm the works in their front. Sir John Hope, however, had now gained the heights commanding Siboure, so that he was in a position to take advantage of any forward movement the right centre of the enemy might make. He kept up this false attack until nightfall, engaging the attention of Reille's and Villatte's Divisions, and thus preventing them from sending succour to the centre of the French Army under Clausel.

While the First and Fifth Divisions held their ground on the left, the rest of the army advanced, and drove the enemy from their several positions along the whole front and seizing the bridges of Ascain and Arnots over the Nivelle. The French retired on all sides, abandoning their entrenched camp of St. Jean de Luz. During the action, Soult arrived with a large body of troops at Serres, and threatened the Allied centre, but the position of Hope's wing prevented his giving any assistance to Clausel, and Sir John followed the retreating French as soon as he could cross the river.

Owing to the duties assigned to the two brigades of Guards, their losses were slight. The total losses during the day's operations however were above 200 killed, and nearly 2,300 wounded.

★★★

On the 10th of November, 1813, while the light companies of the Coldstream and 3rd Guards were skirmishing in front of Irun, the present Sir Wyndham Anstruther, then an officer in the Coldstream Guards, was severely wounded by a musket-ball just below the knee; and had he not received the most unceasing attention from the surgeon, Mr. Rose, he would in all probability have lost his leg. When the army commanded by the Duke of Wellington advanced, in the early part of the spring of 1814, Mr. Rose recommended Mr. Anstruther to return to England on sick leave; and he was placed, on his arrival, under the care of the celebrated surgeon, Sir Everard Home, by whose skill he completely recovered, but was not able to join the British Army before it had reached Paris after the Battle of Waterloo.

Mr. Anstruther remained several months in Paris, and in the early part of 1816, after dining one day with Mr. Boulton, an old friend, who had hired a country-house at St. Maur, two leagues beyond Vincennes, was returning to town in a small carriage upon two wheels, called a *coucou*, commonly used in those days, and which travelled at the rate of about five miles an hour. Having placed himself on the front seat outside with the driver, after a time they got into conversation, and thinking, from his appearance, that he looked like an old soldier, Mr. Anstruther inquired whether he had served; to which the coachman answered in the affirmative, mentioning the number of his regiment and the *battues* in which he had taken part; and he added that he was afraid he had killed an English officer in front of Irun, on the banks of the Bidassoa.

Mr. Anstruther naturally felt surprised at what he had heard, knowing that he was the only officer hit at the time and place specified, so he questioned the driver as to the nature of the ground, and his reasons for being so sure of having killed the officer. The man at once said that about three o'clock on the 10th of November, he and a few comrades ran down from Irun into a small clump of brushwood about half-way between the town and the hedges lined by the English; that they had not been there long before they wounded one of the Englishmen, and that an officer sprang forward to the assistance of the wounded soldier, when he, the coachman, fired and hit the officer, who fell, to all appearance, mortally wounded.

The driver was perfectly astonished when informed that the English officer he thought he had killed was still alive and sitting by his side. The old soldier even shed (or pretended to shed) tears of joy; and after a minute examination of dates and details, Mr. Anstruther presented his *quondam* enemy with a couple of *napoleons* to drink his health. This he did, after placing his carriage in the yard of the village inn, and to some purpose, for he got very drunk, to the amusement of the villagers, to whom he recounted his story, and who carried him in triumph upon their shoulders, crying, "*Vive l'officier Anglais!*"

★★★

The French now retired to the heights of Bidart on the road to Bayonne, and prepared to defend the passage of the Adour, and on the 11th the British Army moved forward. The First Division, after passing over the strongly-fortified position in front of St. Jean de Luz, came in sight of that town about twelve o'clock, and, descending into the valley, and, fording the river above the town, advanced the same afternoon to within eight miles of Bayonne. The First Guards' Brigade took post about one and a half mile distant from, and to the right of, the high road. The enemy's right rested at Anglet; their centre on the ridge of Beyres, and their left on the entrenched camp of Bayonne, near the confluence of the Nive and the Adour.

Bayonne is covered to the south by Vauban's old entrenched camp, and here Soult's right, in three divisions, under Reille, was posted, touching the Lower Adour, and supported by a flotilla. A swamp was in his front, and several fortified posts were pushed forward near Anglet, two miles from Bayonne. Clausel's three divisions extended from the entrenched camp to the Nive, covered partly by the swamp, a fortified house, and an inundation near Urdanis; D'Erlon's four divisions extended up the right bank of the Nive; D'Armanac was in front of Ustaritz and Foy, at Cambo.

Wellington, determining that his position between the Nivelles and the Nive was too contracted, planned to cross the river to establish himself on the left bank of the Adour, but poor weather delayed him so the First Brigade of Guards returned to St. Jean de Luz, where Wellington had now established his headquarters, and were quartered in the suburb of Siboure.

An officer of the Guards, writing from St. Jean de Luz on the 28th of November, after giving an account of the state of affairs, and of the two Brigades of Guards in particular, refers to a report that was current is the town, that Napoleon was coming to Bayonne to take command of the French Armies against Lord Wellington, and he then adds;—

I am sure that there is not a man in the army, from Lord Wellington himself to the lowest soldier, that would not think it the happiest day of his life to be fairly placed in front of the French with Bonaparte at their head. If ever there was a day when British soldiers would be more than themselves, that day would certainly be the one.

That day would not, as it transpired, come very soon—but it would come soon enough.

★★

During the winter of 1813, the Guards were stationed with headquarters at St. Jean de Luz, and most comfortable we managed to make them. For some short time previously, we had been on scanty commons, and had undergone considerable privation: indeed, we might have said, like the colonel to Johnny Newcome on his arrival to join his regiment, "We sons of Mars have long been fed on brandy and cigars."

I had no cause to complain personally; for my servant, a Sicilian, was one of the most accomplished foragers (ill-natured persons might give him a worse name) in the whole army; and when others were nearly starving, he always managed to provide meat or poultry. He rode on his mule sometimes from twenty to thirty miles, often running the greatest dangers, to procure me a good meal; of which he took care to have, very justly, a large share for himself.

At St. Jean de Luz, we were more attentive to our devotions than we had been for some time. Divine service was performed punctually every Sunday on the sand-hills near the town; Lord Wellington and his numerous staff placed themselves in the midst of our square, and his lordship's chaplain read the service, to which Lord Wellington always appeared to listen with great attention.

The mayor of the town, thinking to please "the great English lord," gave a ball at the Hôtel de Ville. Our commander-in-chief did not go, but was represented by Waters. I was there, and expected to see some of the young ladies of the country, so famed for their beauty; they were, however, far too patriotic to appear, and the only lady present was Lady Waldegrave, then living with her husband at headquarters. What was one partner among so many? The ball was a dead failure, in spite of the efforts of the mayor, who danced, to our intense amusement, an English hornpipe, which he had learnt in not a very agreeable manner, *viz.*, when a prisoner of war in the hulks at Plymouth.

There were two packs of hounds at St. Jean de Luz; one kept by Lord Wellington, the other by Marsden, of the commissariat. Our officers went uncommonly straight. Perhaps our best man across country (though sometimes somewhat against his will) was the late Colonel Lascelles of my regiment, then, like myself, a mere lad. He rode a horse seventeen hands high, called *Bucephalus*, which invariably ran away with him, and more than once had nearly capsized Lord Wellington. The good living at St. Jean de Luz agreed so well with my friend that he waxed fat, and from that period to his death was known to the world by the jovial appellation of Bacchus Lascelles.

Here I remember seeing, for the first time, a very remarkable character, the Hon. W. Dawson, of my regiment. He was surrounded by muleteers, with whom he was bargaining to provide carriage for innumerable hampers of wine, liqueurs, hams, potted meat, and other good things which he had brought from England. He was a particularly gentlemanly and amiable man, much beloved by the regiment. No one was so hospitable or lived so magnificently. His cooks were the best in the army, and he, besides, had a host of servants of all nations—Spaniards, French, Portuguese, Italians—who were employed in scouring the country for provisions. Lord Wellington once honoured him with his company; and, on entering the ensign's tent, found him alone at table, with a dinner fit for a king, his plate and linen in good keeping, and his wines perfect.

Lord Wellington was accompanied on this occasion by Sir Edward Pakenham and Colonel du Burgh, afterward Lord Downes. It fell to my lot to partake of his princely hospitality, and dine with him at his quarters, a farmhouse in a village on the Bidassoa, and I never saw a better dinner put upon table. The career of this amiable Amphitryon, to our great regret, was cut short, after exercising for about a year a splendid, but not very wise, hospitality. He had only a younger brother's fortune; his debts became very considerable, and he was obliged to quit the Guards. He and his friends had literally eaten up his little fortune.

★★★

Wellington now proposed to pass the Nive with his right wing, and place it on the Adour, while, to conceal his intentions, Sir John Hope was to make a demonstration with his left wing of 24,000 men, against the entrenched camp at Bayonne, occupied by Reille and Villatte.

The duty assigned to the left wing of the British Army, after reconnoitring the position and strength of the enemy in front of Bayonne, was to examine the mouth of the Lower Adour, with a view to hereafter throwing a bridge across that river. The two Brigades of Guards paraded, at two a.m. on the 9th, and were soon *en route* along the coast road to take up their position. The morning was wet and dreary, and after a fatiguing march, the brigades halted at Barouillet, in front of Bidart, until they were joined by the rest of the division.

★★★

We took our turn of outposts in the neighbourhood of Bidart, a large village, about ten miles from Bayonne. Early one frosty morning in December, an order came, that if we saw the enemy advancing, we were not to fire or give the alarm. About five, we perceived two battalions wearing grenadier caps coming on. They turned out to belong to a Nassau regiment which had occupied the advanced post of the enemy, and, hearing that Napoleon had met with great reverses in Germany, signified to us their intention to desert. They were a fine-looking body of men, and appeared, I thought, rather ashamed of the step they had taken.

On the same day we were relieved, and on our way back met Lord Wellington with his hounds. He was dressed in a light blue frock-coat (the colour of the Hatfield hunt) which had been sent out to him as a present from Lady Salisbury, then one of the leaders of the fashionable world, and an enthusiastic admirer of His Lordship.

The commissary-general, Marsden, who belonged to headquarters, succeeded in collecting from England a kennel of splendid hounds. On the Marquis of Worcester's (the late Duke of Beaufort) leaving the army, he promised to send some of his father's dogs to Marsden; other gentlemen followed this nobleman's example, and before we crossed the Bidassoa the pack was complete, and in fine condition. The hunting in the Pyrenees reminded me of my native Wales; it was all up hill and down dale, and for that reason, when a fox was found, he was seldom if ever killed. The best riders belonging to the hunt were the officers of the 14th and 16th Dragoons, who were, as a rule, well mounted.

I have seen at a meet in the Pyrenees about two hundred officers assembled, some (as I have said) well mounted, but the majority on "screws," ponies, or even mules—a strange contrast to the Quorn and Pytchley gatherings. The greatest character of all as I have noted was Lascelles, on his immense horse, on which he used to delight to race uphill for a lark, and many were the scrapes he got into with the whipper-in for riding over the bounds.

One fine morning in October, 1813, *Monsieur Renard* took it into his head to cross the Bidassoa, and the dogs and huntsman, heedless of danger, followed. The notes of the hounds and the cheering of the huntsman alarmed a French drum-major and some twenty boys whom he was instructing in a secluded spot on the banks of the river. Instead of showing fight, the drum-major with his young pupils scampered off; the dogs, meanwhile, accompanied by the huntsman, were in full cry, and shortly afterwards killed a fine dog fox. The field had remained on our side of the river, enjoying the sport without incurring any danger, when, all of a sudden, the enemy, wondering what the deuce we were about, came down in force, with a battery of field-pieces, and opened fire, which made us all scamper off as if Old Nick had been at our heels.

Marsden, however, advanced to the water's edge, and, with his white pocket handkerchief as a flag of truce, asked permission of the French officer in command to cross and explain what we were doing. This request was acceded to, and, when our gallant foe had heard the reasons why he had advanced out of bounds, he very graciously permitted the huntsman and dogs to recross the river and join us.

★★

The Fifth Division crossed the valley between Biarritz and Bidart, their left resting upon the sea.

At eight o'clock the First Battalion First Guards advanced, covered by the Light Infantry and by the fire of artillery, and became at once engaged; the enemy soon began to retire, contesting every inch of ground, every hedge, and every bank; by one o'clock, the Light Infantry having driven the enemy through the village of Anglet, and down the slopes of the entrenched camp, the First Division gained the heights on the right of the road near that village.

While the attention of the French had been thus engaged with Hope's army. Hill and Beresford were enabled to pass the Nive near Ustaritz and Cambo, when the enemy fell back without resistance, and Wellington having thus succeeded in the object of his attack, *viz.*, the gaining a field for operating against the French left, directed Hope's troops, which had so materially assisted in attaining that object, to commence, about six o'clock in the evening, their return to St. Jean de Luz. The Fifth Division, which formed the rear-guard, halted at Bidart, leaving a Portuguese brigade in advance at Anglet; and the same night the First Brigade of Guards, under Maitland, reached its former quarters at Siboure, the southern suburb of St. Jean de Luz.

★★

When the headquarters of the army were at St. Jean de

Luz, Soult made a movement in front of our right centre, which the English general took for a reconnaissance. As the French general perceived that we had ordered preparations to receive him, he sent a flag of truce to demand a cessation of hostilities, saying that he wanted to shoot an officer and several men for acts of robbery committed by them, with every sort of atrocity, on the farmers and peasantry of the country. The execution took place in view of both armies, and a terrible lesson it was. I cannot specify the date of this event, but think it must have been the latter end of November, 1813.

About the same time General Harispe, who commanded a corps of Basques, issued a proclamation forbidding the peasantry to supply the English with provisions or forage on pain of death; it stated that we were savages, and, as a proof of this, our horses were born with short tails. I saw this absurd proclamation, which was published in French and in the Basque languages, and distributed all over the country.

Among the numerous bad characters in our ranks, several were coiners, or usurers of bad money. In the Second Brigade of Guards, just before we arrived at St. Jean de Luz, a soldier was convicted of this offence, and was sentenced to receive eight hundred lashes. This man, made sham Spanish dollars out of the pewter spoons of the regiment. As he had before been convicted and flogged, he received this terrible sentence and died under the lash. Would it not have been better to have condemned him to be shot? It would have been more humane, certainly more military, and far less brutal.

The light company of my battalion of the 1st Guards, in 1813, rejoiced in a very handsome poodle, which had, if I mistake not, been made prisoner at Vittoria. At the commencement of the battle of the 9th of December, 1813, near the mayor's house, not far from Bidart, we observed the gallant Frederick Ponsonby well in front with skirmishers, and by the side of his horse the soldiers' poodle. The colonel was encouraging our men to advance; and the poodle, in great glee, was jumping and barking at the bullets, as they flew round him like hail.

On a sudden, we observed Ponsonby struggling with a French mounted officer, whom he had already disarmed, and was endeavouring to lead off to our lines; when the French skirmishers, whose numbers had increased, fired several shots, and wounded Ponsonby, forcing him to relinquish his prisoner and to retire. At the same time, a bullet broke one of the poor dog's legs. For his gallant conduct in this affair, the poodle became, if possible, a still greater favourite than he was before; and his friends, the men of the light company, took him to England, where I saw my three-legged friend for several years afterward, the most prosperous of poodles, and the happiest of the canine race.

★★

Wellington's left was now separated from the rest of his army by the Nive, and Soult was not slow in seizing his opportunity. He advanced from Bayonne on the morning of the 10th of December, at the head of 60,000 men, against Hope's wing. Reille, driving the Portuguese from Anglet, advanced towards Barouillet, while Clausel on his left attacked Arcange, occupied by Kempts' Brigade of the Light Division, who maintained their position all day. The sound of heavy firing in front, and the arrival of an *aide-de-camp*, warning the Guards and the troops in rear, that the attack was serious, the Guards pushed on rapidly to the scene of action, and took their place in line; but the state of the ground having prevented the enemy deploying his forces, the attack was already repulsed, and a renewal of it was prevented by the arrival of three divisions near Ustaritz, on the left of the enemy's attack. The First Brigade, however, remained that night in Bidart.

The French again attacked the outposts of the left wing on the 11th, and penetrated the first line; but when Aylmer's brigade arrived on the ground, Soult withdrew his troops behind the Etang de Chartreuse, opposite Barouillet. The Guards relieved the 5th Division in front line that night, the latter forming on the same ground from which the Guards had moved. The

Bayonne from the sandhills

two Brigades of Guards at once took up a position in front of Barouillet, the First Brigade, under Maitland, being near a farm-house on the brow of a hill, separated by a narrow ravine from the heights which had so often been the scene of contest, and which were still held by the French.

The picquets of the Third Battalion First Guards were posted in a thick coppice wood on the slopes of the hill, while those of the first, on the extreme right, commanded by Captain West, were in a large orchard to the right of the farmhouse. The First Battalion First Guards, under Colonel Askew, was formed on the high ground to the rear, while the Third Battalion, under Colonel Stuart, was to the left, in rear of the farm, with some artillery. A picquet of the First Guards, under Lord Saltoun, occupied a hut to the left, to watch the road which led from the enemy's position, and to keep up the communication with the Second Brigade, in front of the mayor's house.

★★★

During the action of the 10th of December, 1813, commonly known as that of the mayor's house, in the neighbourhood of Bayonne, the Grenadier Guards, under the command of Colonel Tynling (Tinling), occupied an unfinished redoubt on the right of the high road. The Duke of Wellington happened to pass with Freemantle and Lord A. Hill, on his return to headquarters, having satisfied himself that the fighting was merely a feint on the part of Soult. His Grace, on looking around, saw, to his surprise, a great many umbrellas, with which the officers protected themselves from the rain that was then falling.

Arthur Hill came galloping up to us, saying, "Lord Wellington does not approve of the use of umbrellas during the enemy's firing, and will not allow 'the gentlemen's sons? to make themselves ridiculous in the eyes of the army." ("They are worthy the name given them by the army, that of gentlemen's sons.)" Colonel Tynling, a few days afterward, received a wigging from Lord Wellington for suffering his officers to carry umbrellas in the face of the enemy; his lordship observing: "The Guards may in uniform, when on duty at St. James's, carry them if they please; but in the field it is not only ridiculous but unmilitary."

★★

The night of the 11th was dark and wet, and when morning broke the French appeared in great force, and more troops were coming up. About ten o'clock, a strong line of *tirailleurs* was seen advancing from the west along the brow of the ravine in front of Maitland's First Brigade of Guards; the artillery opened fire; and, the outposts becoming engaged, the skirmishing was kept up during the greater part of the day in front of both Brigades, causing a loss of about 200 officers and men. Lieutenant-Colonel Coote Martin, commanding the picquets of the First Battalion, First Guards, was shot while giving some directions in the orchard, and almost immediately afterwards Captain Thompson, of the same battalion, an officer of much promise, fell mortally wounded, while leading on his men.

Marshal Soult, finding he could make no impression on the allied left and that the British position on the left bank of the Nive was secure, and believing that they would be occupied in strengthening it still further, retired behind his entrenchments; but he was not without hope of eventual success, and though he had so far failed, he resolved, after leaving only a cordon of outposts in front of our troops, to pass 35,000 men quickly through Bayonne during the night, with the intention of attacking Hill's corps the following morning on the right of the Nive,

The British general, however, in expectation of such an attack, sent Marshal Beresford, with three divisions, early in the morning of the 13th, to Hill's assistance. That general had only 14,000 men under him, but he held his ground at St. Pierre, and repelled every attack until the three divisions arrived, with Wellington at their head.

The French attacks then became gradually feebler, and at two o'clock Wellington ordered a general advance; the French retreated fighting, and during the night Foy's division retired across the Adour, and were sent to reinforce Reille, opposed to the British left. While the fight was raging at St. Pierre, on the 13th, the enemy reinforced their advanced posts in front of the First and Fifth Divisions, and firing was kept up with little intermission till the afternoon. The First Brigade of Guards, the Coldstreams, and Lord Aylmer's Brigade were those chiefly engaged. Captain Carey le Marchant, of the 1st Guards, *aide-de-camp* to Lieutenant-General Sir William Stewart, was severely wounded.

★★

We expected to remain quietly in our winter quarters at St. Jean de Luz, but to our surprise, early one morning, we were aroused from sleep by the beating of the drum calling us to arms. We were soon in marching order. It appeared that our outposts had been severely pushed by the French, and we were called upon to support our companions in arms.

The whole of the British Army, as well as the division of the Guards, had commenced a forward movement. Soult, seeing this, entirely changed his tactics, and from that time, viz., the ninth of December, a series of engagements took place. The fighting on the ninth was comparatively insignificant. When we were attacked on the tenth, the Guards held the mayor's house and the grounds and orchards attached; this was an important station.

Large bodies of the enemy's infantry approached, and, after desultory fighting, succeeded in penetrating our position, when many hand-to-hand combats ensued. Toward the afternoon, officers and men having displayed great gallantry, we drove the enemy from the ground which they courageously disputed with us, and from which they eventually retreated to Bayonne. Every day there was constant fighting along the whole of our line, which extended from the sea to the Lower Pyrenees—a distance probably not less than thirty miles.

On the 11th we only exchanged a few shots, but on the 12th, Soult brought into action from fifteen to twenty thousand men, and attacked our left with a view of breaking our line. One of the most remarkable incidents of the 12th was the fact of an English battalion being surrounded by a division of French in the neighbourhood of the mayor's house, which, as before observed, was one of our principal strategical positions. The French commanding officer, believing that no attempt would be made to resist, galloped up to the officer of the British regiment and demanded his sword.

Upon this, without the least hesitation, the British officer shouted out, "This fellow wants us to surrender: charge, my boys! and show them what stuff we are made of." Instantaneously a hearty cheer rang out, and our men rushed forward impetuously, drove off the enemy at the point of the bayonet, and soon disposed of the surrounding masses. In a few minutes, they had taken prisoners, or killed, the whole of the infantry regiment opposed to them.

On the 13th was fought the bloody Battle of the Nivelle. Soult had determined to make a gigantic effort to drive us back into Spain. During the night of the 12th, he rapidly concentrated about sixty thousand troops in front of Sir Rowland Hill's *corps d'armée*, consisting of fifteen thousand men, who occupied a very strong position, which was defended by some of the best artillery in the world. At daybreak Sir Rowland Hill was astonished to find himself threatened by masses of infantry advancing over a country luckily intersected by rivulets, hedges, and woods, which prevented the enemy from making a rapid advance; whilst, at the same time, it was impossible on such ground to employ cavalry.

Sir Rowland, availing himself of an elevated position, hurriedly surveyed his ground, and concentrated his men at such points as he knew the nature of the field would induce the enemy to attack. The French, confident of success from their superior numbers, came gallantly up, using the bayonet for the first time in a premeditated attack. Our men stood their ground, and for hours acted purely on the defensive; being sustained by the admirable practice of our artillery, whose movements no difficulty of ground could, on this occasion, impede, so efficiently were the guns horsed, and so perfect was the training of the officers. It was not until mid-day that the enemy became discouraged at finding that they were unable to make any serious impression on our position; they then retired in good order, Sir Rowland Hill not daring to follow them.

Lord Wellington arrived just in time to witness the end of the battle; and while going over the field with Sir Rowland Hill, he remarked that he had never seen so many men *hors de combat* in so small a space.

I must not omit to mention a circumstance which occurred during this great fight, alike illustrative of cowardice and of courage. The colonel of an infantry regiment, who shall be nameless, being hard pressed, showed a disposition not only to run away himself, but to order his regiment to retire. In fact, a retrograde movement had commenced, when my gallant and dear friend Lord Charles Churchill, *aide-de-camp* to Sir William Stewart, dashed forward, and, seizing the colours of the regiment, exclaimed, "If your colonel will not lead you, follow me, my boys!" The gallantry of this youth, then only eighteen years of age, so animated the regiment and restored their confidence, that they rallied and shared in the glory of the day.

One of the other heroes of that bloody day was Frank Russell, "the Pride of Woburn Abbey," whose character it would be as difficult to overestimate as it would be to give an idea of his chivalrous bearing in presence of the enemy. He possessed all the requisites for a good soldier. Of noble birth, good-looking, and with a splendid figure, he was valiant in the extreme. He was gazetted in the 7th Fusiliers at the age of sixteen, and forthwith sent with them to Spain, where he followed the fortunes of his corps up to the time of the battle of the Pyrenees. One of the most furious attacks made by Soult on our position at this celebrated conflict was directed on the left wing of the British Army. The fusiliers were posted on the right, and ordered to maintain themselves against all odds, and not to budge a foot. The French general, being determined to turn our right, sent an overwhelming force against Frank's regiment, which was posted against a mountain wall.

The fusiliers defended themselves with obstinate courage, but their colonel, for some reason which was never explained, declared it prudent to order a retreat, though his line was unbroken. Frank Russell, however, shouted out, "Not yet, colonel," and, with the colours of his regiment, mounted the wall and cheered our men on, the French meanwhile renewing their attack with redoubled vigour. During this fierce struggle, however, our hero kept his position till the fierce energy with which the French had been fighting began to cool, for Wellington had meanwhile broken Soult's centre, and the retreat of the French forces was ordered. Before Russell quitted his post of honour, Lord Wellington with his staff happened to pass by the wall, and saw Russell standing on the wall, holding the colours of his regiment, which were riddled with bulletholes. On the following day, when the gallant young officer's conduct was reported to our great commander, he exclaimed, "Ah! there's nothing like blood."

★★★

The First Brigade of Guards returned to St. Jean de Luz after these several actions, and as the enemy made no further attempts during the remainder of the year 1813 to molest the British, the beginning of the following year found the Allied Armies firmly established on French soil. Soult employed himself during the subsequent short period of inaction in strengthening his position, protecting the passages of the Rivers Bidouse and Gave d'Oleron, and making demonstrations.

On the 3rd of January, 1814, he attacked the British position on the Joyeuse, and shortly after appeared in force in front of the left wing. The Brigades of Guards were immediately despatched from St. Jean de Luz to the outposts of Barouillet, where they relieved the Fifth Division, which then took ground to the right. As no attack however, was made by the French, the Guards returned to St. Jean de Luz, leaving Lord Aylmer's brigade in charge of the outposts. On the 14th of January this brigade was relieved by the First Guards, who in succession were relieved by the Second Brigade.

The soldiers on outpost-duty were employed in constructing a line of entrenchments along the front of the left wing, for the defence of the ground behind Barouillet, and this duty was performed by the several battalions in rotation for three days each, but was much impeded by the wet and stormy weather that prevailed during the whole month.

The left wing of the army was now destined for the investment of Bayonne, and although this duty prevented their taking part in the operations under Wellington's immediate command, which led to the several actions of Orthez, Garris, Aire, and Tarbes, during the forward movement of the right and centre of the army towards Toulouse, the duties assigned to it were of no less importance.

★★

Whilst these operations were going on, Soult was organising his discouraged army, in order to make, as early as possible, another convenient stand. The enemy fell back on Orthes, and there took up a strong position; Soult was, nevertheless, destined to be beaten again at Orthes. It so happened that, for the first time since the Battle of Vittoria, our cavalry were engaged: the nature of the ground at Nive and Nivelle was such as to prevent the possibility of employing the mounted soldier.

I must here record an incident which created a considerable sensation in military circles in connection with the battle of Orthes. The 10th Hussars, officered exclusively by men belonging to the noblest families of Great Britain, showed a desire to take a more active part in the contest than their colonel (Quintin) thought prudent. They pressed hard to be permitted to charge the French cavalry on more than one occasion, but in vain. This so disgusted every officer in the regiment, that they eventually signed a round robin, by which they agreed

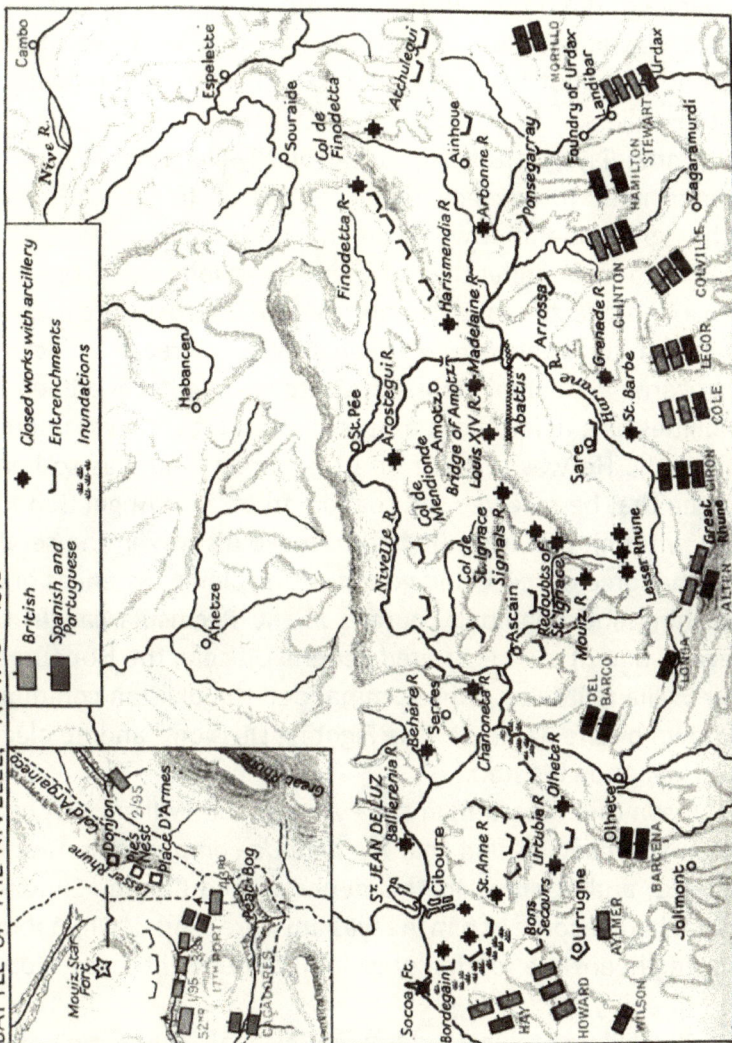

BATTLE OF THE NIVELLE, NOV. 10TH 1813

Legend:
- British
- Spanish and Portuguese
- Closed works with artillery
- Entrenchments
- Inundations

Cambo, Espelette, Souraide, Achulegui, Col de Finodetta, Ainhoue, Arbonne R., Mortilo, Foundry of Urdax, Iandibar, Urdax, Hamilton, Stewart, Finodetta R., Harismendia R., St. Pée, Arostegui R., Madelaine R., Clinton, Colville, Zagaramurdi, Habancen, Col de Mendionde, Amotz, Louis XIV R., Signals R., Abatis, Arrosse R., Hurs Grenade R., St. Barbe, Lecor, Cole, Ahetze, Col de St. Ignace, Sare, Lesser Rhune, Giron, Ascain, Redoubts of St. Ignace, Mouiz R., Del Barco, Great Rhune, Alten, Loriga, Behère R., Serres, Chamoneta R., Olhete R., St. Jean de Luz, Ballerenia R., Ciboure, St. Anne R., Urtubia R., Olhete, Bons Secours, Urrugne, Olhete, Barrena, Jolimont, Socoa Fc., Bordegain, Hay, Howard, Aylmer, Wilson, Nive R., Nivelle R.

Inset map: Mouiz Star Fort, Greater Rhune, Lesser Rhune, Doujon, Ness, Place D'Armes, Great Bog, Little Bog, 2/95, 1/95, 52nd, 17th Port., Cacabeles

Niv-e R.

never again to speak to their colonel. When the regiment returned to England a court of inquiry was held, which resulted, through the protection of the prince regent, in the colonel's exoneration from all blame, and at the same time the exchange of the rebellious officers into other regiments.

It was at the Battle of Orthes that the late Duke of Richmond was shot through the body, gallantly fighting with the 7th Fusiliers.

Immediately after the Battle of Nivelle, Lord Wellington determined to advance his whole line on to French ground. The right, under his own command, pushed on toward Orthes, whilst the left, under the command of Sir John Hope, proceeded in the direction of Bayonne. We (the Guards) were incorporated in the latter *corps d'armée*. However, I recall an incident concerning General Gabriel. Whatever might have been his abilities as a field officer, as a soldier his bravery was unquestionable. He was the son of a clergyman, and was so handsome that he received the cognomen of "The Angel Gabriel." On entering the army, he had to make his way in the service by the force of merit and good fortune alone. Instances of his dashing and headlong courage in the Peninsula caught the eye of one of our celebrated general officers, the Honourable Sir William Stewart, who commanded the division commonly known by the name of "The Fighting Division," and he placed Gabriel upon his staff.

Upon one occasion, in the Pyrenees, Sir William was not a little surprised to find that his *aide-de-camp* was *non est inventus*, and upon asking his nephew, Lord Charles Churchill, what had become of him, he was answered thus: "Oh, Gabriel, having heard the roaring of cannon to our right, has galloped off to enjoy the fun."

Sir William Stewart, addressing his staff, said: "Well, then, we cannot do better than follow him;" and off they went. On reaching the pass of Roncesvalles, to their astonishment they saw Gabriel, at the head of a few stragglers whom he had picked up on the way, charge a bridge which the enemy were crossing, and completely rout them. Sir William Stewart was so delighted with this act of daring bravery, that he recommended his young *aide-de-camp* for promotion, which the Duke of Wellington ratified in one of his earliest despatches.

★★★

The light companies of the Brigade of Guards were now placed under the command of Lieutenant-Colonel Lord Saltoun, who had been promoted to a company at the end of the year 1813. This promotion would have sent him to the home battalion, but, anxious to continue on active service, he applied for, and at the beginning of February, 1814, received, the above command, which he retained with great credit to himself to the end of the war.

(Readers wishing to discover further details of the career of Lord Saltoun will find them within, 'The March to Hougoumont' by John H. Lewis.)

Wellington had for some time been planning an expedition worthy of his reputation. He believed that Soult was convinced that the British Army could not pass the Adour, and least of all, that the attempt could be made at its mouth: nevertheless, it was here that the British general had decided to make the attempt. For this purpose, he collected at Socoa, near St. Jean de Luz, forty of the ordinary French trading vessels, or *Chasses-Marées*, ostensibly—it was circulated—for commissariat purposes, and loaded them with materials for constructing a bridge of boats.

With a view to concealing his design, and while Hope, with his left wing, showed a bold front towards Bayonne, Hill was directed, in the second week of February, to take advantage of a sharp frost to attack the enemy. He did so on the 16th, driving the French advanced posts back to St. Palais, on the Upper Bidouse, whereupon Soult retreated behind the Gave d'Oleron, with his left resting on Navarreins, leaving a strong garrison under Thouvenot in Bayonne.

While the arrangements for the passage of the Adour were being completed, the two Brigades of Guards, under Maitland and Stopford, advanced, on the 15th of February, to the plateau

Bridge of boats across the Adour below Bayonne

near Biaritz, and took up a position facing the town with the rest of Hope's troops; the first Brigade, on the right of the road to Bayonne, occupying, with a detachment, the *château* of Pucho; the 5th Division, on their right, extending from Bussussary to the Nive, while Hinuber's Germans and Stopford's Second Guards' Brigade were on the left.

The light Companies of the Guards, and the light battalions of the German Legion, were on the advanced posts; the sentries of the First Brigade being posted a short distance from Anglet, which was occupied by the enemy; while Aylmer's brigade with Campbell's Portuguese were in support at Bidart.

★★★

Early in the spring of 1814 I was ordered to proceed with Lord James Hay on a foraging expedition. Our party consisted of fifty men, armed with firelocks, and mounted upon mules. It would be impossible to give any adequate idea of our zigzag march, and our wanderings in the dark; at last, after proceeding in tolerably good order for about nine hours, we came in sight of a village called Dax, consisting of a few pretty houses, about a mile distant. At break of day, wanting our accustomed breakfast, we determined to seek quarters there; but gave directions to the non-commissioned officers to prevent the slightest disorder or pillage. My batman, Proyd, who spoke nearly every European language, advanced into the market-place with a saucepan, which he had brought with him from camp, and began striking it with a thick stick with all his might.

The noise awoke the inhabitants, some of whom approached our party, and, after much persuasion, one of them was prevailed upon by Lord James to show us the mayor's house; and presently this personage, "dressed in a little brief authority," made his appearance. We told him that one object of our coming was to procure provisions for ourselves, and forage for our horses and mules, but that everything supplied should be paid for. The mayor regarded us with suspicion, until Proyd entered with our teacups and boiling water, and asked in good French for some plates for "My Lord." The title of "My Lord" electrified the mayor, and in less than a quarter of an hour the whole of his family appeared, and offered us and our men everything that we required.

With a heart full of thankfulness, I sat down to an excellent breakfast of cold meat, eggs, coffee, and bread and butter; and to crown all, one of the daughters of the mayor, an extremely elegant young lady, entered the room with some delicious comfitures, of which she said her mother begged our acceptance. The wife of the mayor soon after joined us, and, to our astonishment and delight, began conversing with us in English. She said that she had been brought up in England, and that her mother was English, but had left her native land for France when she was about sixteen.

Having refreshed ourselves, and seen that the horses and mules had been properly groomed and baited, we gave orders to return, and our troop put itself again in motion; the animals being laden with straw, Indian corn, and forage of every description, for which we paid the mayor in Spanish dollars. After we had marched some hours, finding that, hampered as we were, we could not march well in the dark, we determined to halt at the first village we fell in with, and continue our march the next morning to Bayonne; whence we were then about eight leagues distant. We soon struck a little *bourg* about two leagues from Dax, but could see no one stirring in the place; in fact, it seemed deserted.

However, Proyd, ever alert, heard a dog bark in one of the houses, a sign that the inhabitants were hiding. We knocked first at one house and then at another, until our patience began to be exhausted, when a sleepy-looking fellow popped his head out of a window, and asked us in a most insolent manner what we wanted. While we were parleying with him, one of the sergeants, an active young fellow, scrambled up to the window from whence this Caliban was jeering at us, bolted down the stairs, opened the front door, and admitted us into the house.

It turned out to be the cabaret of the village, and it was the landlord who had just greeted us in this abusive manner. He was evidently an inveterate enemy of the British, for he would neither give us any information as to how our men were to be billeted, nor show us even common civility. However, finding our host so contumacious, we ordered him to be placed in *durance vile*, determining to carry him off to headquarters as a prisoner.

The next morning a council of war was held to devise a plan for transporting our prisoner. Proyd, the *figaro* of the party, suggested placing him upon a mule; but the question was, how to get him mounted on the back of one at so early an hour in the morning, without creating a disturbance in the village. Hay, however, had no scruples on that score, and gave instructions to have the prisoner tied upon one of the animals. Proyd, approaching the fellow from behind, threw one of the regimental bags over his head, and with the aid of his comrades fastened him securely on a mule. When all was arranged to our satisfaction, the man began to bellow, and his neighbour, finding we were in earnest, came out and begged for mercy; but to no purpose, for we were determined to make an example of the disobliging brute; so off we started with our prisoner.

We arrived in camp just in time to report the result of our expedition to the commanding officer, who was much amused at our bringing, in addition to an ample supply of forage, etc., an impertinent fellow, with his head tied up in a bag. The next morning, after a severe lecture, our prisoner received his *congé*, and was desired to return home and tell his friends that we differed entirely from other soldiers who had occupied the country, for we paid ready money for everything we required, and expected to be treated with civility by the inhabitants.

A few days afterward, another foraging party was organised, and on their arrival at the same village every door was opened, and provisions, corn, hay, etc., offered in abundance, while the greatest civility was paid to our men. The proprietor of the inn was foremost in proffering his services, and expressed his regret for what had occurred before, stating that the cause of it was that, in the dark, the inhabitants mistaking us for a body of men belonging to the Spanish Army, had fled; as a party of soldiers belonging to that nation had a short time before robbed them of their pigs, poultry, and linen, and ill-treated their wives and daughters. After this, our soldiers, when on foraging expeditions, were ordered to dress in uniform, to show the country-people that they belonged to the British Army.

★★★

A week later, all arrangements for forcing the passage of the river completed. Sir John Hope, at midnight, on the 22nd of February, advanced, with 28,000 men, including the two Brigades of Guards, twenty guns, a rocket troop, and eighteen pontoons. On approaching Anglet, the first division turned to the left towards the coast, in strict silence, for although the night was dark, they were within musket shot of the enemy's sentries. The lane by which they were moving was narrow and muddy, with deep ditches on either side, and their progress was delayed for a time by the upsetting of an 18-pounder cannon. Stopford's and Hinuber's Brigades proceeded to the mouth of the river with the pontoons, and at daybreak the light infantry of the First Guards advanced along the plateau, driving the enemy from Anglet into their camp.

Maitland's Brigade followed, advancing through the Bois de Bayonne, dragging the 18-pounders with them, and emerged near to the eastern beacon. Here they formed under cover of the sand hills, close to the marsh, on the west front of the enemy's camp, opposite Boucant. The guns were put in position on the extreme left, near the Adour, fronting the right flank of the enemy's camp. The First Guards, with their guns, were now in a position both to resist any attempt of the enemy to disturb the formation of the bridge, and to cover the subsequent crossing of it. On the appearance of this column the enemy's gunboats and a frigate opened fire, but they were soon driven higher up the river by the fire of the battery and rocket troop.

It was intended that the arrival of the *Chasses-Marées* from Socoa, and the column with the pontoons, should be simultaneous, but the boats were delayed by bad weather. Sir John Hope, however, determined to cross over at once with the means he had at hand. Whilethe attention of the enemy was fixed upon the movements of the First Brigade in their front, a pontoon raft was formed, which, together with available some boats, six companies of the Third Guards, two of the Coldstreams, and two of the 60th, under Stopford were ferried over to the right bank and landed without opposition.

The French, under General Thouvenot, came up a little before dark, their drums beating the *pas de charge*, but they were challenged by Stopford's men, who, waiting until they were close, delivered a rolling fire to their front, while the rocket troop and guns on the sand hills on the southern bank opened fire upon their left flank. The enemy were routed, and on the following morning, the 24th, the remainder of the Second Brigade of Guards, the Germans, and Portuguese crossed over under cover, both of their comrades who had preceded them, and of the First Guards who still remained on the south bank, to prevent any interruption by a sortie from the town.

The flotilla of *Chasses-Marées* appeared in the Adour about noon of the 24th, so the construction of the bridge was immediately begun, the boats were anchored forty feet apart, about three miles below Bayonne, and the bridge was completed unopposed.

While the work was in progress the First Brigade of Guards, after showing a front towards Bayonne, were the last of the First Division to cross over, not by the new bridge, but by the same temporary means employed by their comrades on the previous day—a tedious operation, for only twelve men could cross at a time in one of the pontoon boats, the rapidity of the tide rendering the pontoon raft useless. It was dark before the last men of the brigade were ferried over, and it was not without much difficulty that the last boats were prevented from drifting out to sea.

★★★

Lord Wellington had determined to cross the Adour, and Sir John Hope was entrusted with a *corps d'armée*, which was the first to perform this difficult operation. It was necessary to provide Sir John Hope with a number of small boats; these were accordingly brought on the backs of mules from various Spanish ports, it being impossible, on account of the surf at the entrance of the Adour, as well as the command which the French held of that river, for Lord Wellington to avail himself of water carriage. Soult had given orders for the forces under General Thevenot to dispute the passage.

The first operations of our corps were to throw over the 3rd Guards, under the command of the gallant Colonel Stopford; this was not accomplished without much difficulty: but it was imperatively necessary, in order to protect the point where the construction of the bridge of boats would terminate. They had not been long on the French side of the river before a considerable body of men were seen issuing from Bayonne. Sir John Hope ordered our artillery, and rockets, then for the first time employed, to support our small band. Three or four regiments of French infantry were approaching rapidly, when a well-directed fire of rockets fell amongst them. The consternation of the Frenchmen was such, when these hissing, serpent-like projectiles descended, that a panic ensued, and they retreated upon Bayonne. The next day the bridge of boats was completed, and the whole army crossed.

★★★★★★★★★★★★★★★★★★★★★★★★★★★★★★★★

Sir John Hope lost no time in investing the citadel lying on the right bank of the river, a bend in which favoured the operation by shortening the extent of ground to be occupied, and a marsh partly protected the line he took up. At seven o'clock on the morning of the 25th of February, the First Division and

Bradford's Portuguese advanced towards the citadel in battalion columns of companies, each brigade at deploying distance. The First Guards on the right, with their right resting on the Adour, halted for a short time at Boucant, while the centre and left brigades moved gradually round, forming in succession to their right, till the extreme left rested on the Adour above the town. While this was going on to the north of the river, the Fifth Division, which still remained on the south bank, crossed the Nive, and took up a position between the Nive and the Adour, thus completing the investment, and severing all communication between the town and country.

An attack was also made on the enemy's entrenched camp, to prevent the garrison from interfering with the construction of the bridge, which was completed by the morning of the 26th, and it continued to be used by the Allies till the end of the war as the principal means of communication between the Spanish frontier and Bordeaux.

No sooner was the bridge secure, than Sir John Hope determined to contract his lines round the citadel. The enemy had strongly entrenched himself in the village of St. Etienne, situated on a ridge, along which ran the roads from Bordeaux and Peyhorrada; and this village was further protected by the fire from the fort.

The troops moved forward in three columns, converging on the citadel. The right column, consisting of the two battalions First Guards, advanced in *echelon* of battalions from the left; the Third Battalion leading, halted for a time on the slope of some high ground, when, upon a pre-concerted signal of the display of the Third Battalion Colours, the First Battalion advanced also; the enemy immediately opened fire, and as soon as the First Battalion had crossed a marshy ground in its front, Maitland moved his whole brigade forward together, covered by Light Infantry, and drove the enemy within their entrenchments.

The brigade was now within 900 yards of the citadel, the right resting on the Adour, at the Convent of St. Bernard, which, on being occupied by the light companies of the First Regiment, was converted into a strong post by their commanding officer, Lord Saltoun, it being supposed that the enemy would make a vigorous sortie to attempt to retake it, and destroy the bridge of boats. The left column, consisting of the Second Brigade of Guards, was equally successful in taking up its advanced position; the centre, which moved forward upon the village of St. Etienne, met with considerable opposition, but the French were eventually beat back into the citadel, with the loss of one of their guns.

★★★

After our *corps d'armée*, under the command of Sir John Hope, had crossed the Adour, we were ordered to advance as close as possible under the walls of the town. Accordingly, after suffering considerable loss, we succeeded in investing the town and fortress. The enemy, not contented with firing from the batteries, actually brought a nine-pounder on to the high-road, half-way from their stronghold. This gun did us great injury, and I was witness to a very gallant act of some of the infantry of the German Legion, which effectually stopped any further loss. Captain Wilding, who commanded a company of Hanoverians, suddenly dashed out of a burial-ground to the left of the road, rushed upon the gunners, bayoneted them, and brought the gun in triumph into our lines, amidst the loud cheers of our soldiers.

In this gallant exploit Captain Wilding was badly wounded in the leg, and was obliged to return to England for his recovery; but prior to his removal he had the satisfaction to see, in general orders, the approval, by the commander-in-chief, of his gallant bearing in the capture of the gun. Captain Wilding was a Hanoverian, and brother of Prince Butera, heir to part of whose vast estates in Sicily he succeeded, and is now known by the title of Prince Radali, which was bestowed upon him by the old King of Naples.

Bayonne was eventually invested after a contest, in which it was supposed our loss exceeded five hundred or six hundred men. Here we remained in camp about six weeks, expecting to besiege the citadel; but this event never came off

★★

During the month of March Sir John Hope made every preparation for an attack upon the works, but no heavy artillery arrived. Every house had been turned into an entrenched post, which was the more necessary as, from the accuracy of the French gunners, no sentry could expose himself with impunity.

★★

I may here recount an instance of the folly and foolhardiness of youth, and the recklessness to which a long course of exposure to danger produces. When Bayonne was invested, I was one night on duty on the outer picket. The ground inside the breastwork which had been thrown up for our protection by Burgoyne was in a most disagreeable state for anyone who wished to repose after the fatigues of the day, being knee deep in mud of a remarkably plastic nature. I was dead tired, and determined to get a little rest in some more agreeable spot; so, calling my sergeant, I told him to give me his knapsack for a pillow; I would make a comfortable night of it on the top of the breastwork, as it was an invitingly dry place.

"For heaven's sake, take care, sir," said he; "you'll have fifty bullets in you; you will be killed to a certainty."

"Pooh, nonsense," said I, and climbing up, I wrapped myself in my cloak, laid my head on the knapsack, and soon fell into a sound sleep.

By the mercy of Providence, I remained in a whole skin, either from the French immediately underneath not perceiving me or not thinking me worth a shot; but when General Stopford came up with Lord James Hay (who not long since reminded me of this youthful escapade), I received a severe wigging, and was told to consider myself lucky that I was not put under arrest for exposing my life in so foolish a manner.

It (later) fell to my lot to be on outpost duty, and I then

and there saw a long shot fired from one of our old muskets which showed that Brown Bess, though not equalling our modern weapons, had yet some good solid merits of her own, and when held straight was not to be despised even at a long range. Several shots had been fired from the French pickets, when Captain Grant of the 1st Foot Guards, being the senior officer on duty, came to me to inquire the cause of the firing, and desired me to make my way to the front and endeavour to ascertain what had occurred. Having arrived near the ravine which separated us from the French, I stumbled upon an advanced sentry, a German, who was coolly smoking his pipe. I asked him whether the shots that had been heard came from his neighbourhood, upon which he replied in broken English, "Yes, zir, that feelow you see yonder has fired nine times at mine target (meaning his body), but has missed. I hopes you, *capitaine*, will let me have one shot at him."

The distance between the French picket and ours could not have been less than four hundred yards; so, without giving myself time to think, I said: "Yes, you can have one shot at him." He levelled his musket, fired, and killed his man; whereupon, a sergeant, and two or three French soldiers who had seen him fall, ran down to the front and removed the body.

★★★

As Bordeaux and the adjacent country was ready to declare for the Bourbons, Wellington on the 8th of March, despatched Beresford with a force to that city, which he entered on the 12th, and was well received by the municipality. After remaining there a few days, Beresford left Lord Dalhousie with the Seventh Division, and rejoined his chief on the 18th, *viâ* Bigorre. Wellington, after driving the enemy in a hardly-contested action from Tarbes, continued his advance by easy marches, arriving on the left bank of the Garonne above Toulouse on the 27th, where Soult had entrenched himself upon ground already strong by nature.

While these events were occurring in the south of France, in the north the plains of Champagne had become, since the beginning of the year, the theatre of a desperate struggle, and France was now experiencing an enemy on her own soil. The military genius of Napoleon was never more apparent than when he was commanding inferior forces against the overwhelming numbers of the enemy. Engaging his opponents in detail, and constantly victorious to no permanent beneficial result, he fought on though to a more certain ruin. He left Paris on the 27th of January, and though beaten at La Rothiére on the 1st of February, he was victorious on several other occasions during the month.

On the 21st, at Arcis sur Aube, with 55,000 men, he received 100,000 of the Allies, and retired without confusion behind the Aube. As a last resource he moved north, in order to reinforce his army by the garrisons of the frontier, thus leaving Paris open, and entrusting its defence to the questionable abilities of his brother, Joseph. The Allies then advanced with 250,000 men, arriving before the city on the 29th of March. Two days later Paris capitulated. Napoleon, on receiving this fell news, retired to Fontainebleau, and, after several fruitless attempts at negotiation, abdicated the throne of France on the 6th of April.

Two military events, however, occurred in the south of France in the interval between the emperor's abdication and the receipt of official information of the cessation of hostilities. The Battle of Toulouse was fought, and the sortie from Bayonne, in both of which many lives were fruitlessly sacrificed on both sides.

On the 10th April, four days after the emperor's abdication, the Allies stormed the fortified heights, and drove the French before them. On the 11th, Soult abandoned the town, and on the following morning Wellington entered it in triumph. On the same afternoon messengers arrived announcing the deposition of the emperor, from whom also came a formal injunction to his generals to stop all further hostilities.

★★★

Sir John Hope, who commanded our *corps d'armée* at Bayonne, had his quarters at a village on the Adour, called Beaucauld. He was good enough to name me to the command of the village; which honour I did not hold many days. The enemy made an unexpected sortie, and surrounded General Sir John Hope, when he and the whole of his staff were taken prisoners. The French killed and wounded about one thousand men on this occasion.

The hardly contested Battle of Toulouse was fought about this period, but the Guards were not present to share the honours of a contest which closed the eventful war of the Spanish Peninsula.

★★★

Sir John Hope, while still investing Bayonne, had received information, on the 7th of April, of the fall of Paris; and though it was not sufficiently authoritative to warrant his making a formal communication to the governor, he made it known at the outposts in the belief this would prevent further fruitless loss of life. The French commander, however, paid no attention to the notice, thinking might be a ruse intended to deceive him. Another week elapsed when, at one o'clock on the morning of the 14th of April, a deserter from the citadel informed General Hay, whose brigade of the Fifth Division had been recently removed to the right bank, and who was, on this night. Major-General in charge of the outposts, that a sortie was from the citadel was imminent. Hay at once sent the man to General Hinuber, who put his brigade under arms, and forwarded the intelligence to Sir John Hope, and ordered his own brigade to form at Boucant, in case of alarm.

A strong force of about 3,000 Frenchmen, under cover of the guns from the ramparts, sallied out of the citadel, as forecast, at about three o'clock on the morning of the 14th, and vigorously attacked the picquets of the left and centre of the allied investing force, these being furnished respectively by General Hay's brigade and by the Second Brigade of Guards. The picquets of the First Guards covered the right of the line. It was so dark that it was impossible to tell friend from foe. On the left the rush was so sudden that the enemy quickly carried the church and village, except one house, held by a detachment of the 38th Regiment, which was maintained, until the Germans, in company with Hay's brigade, which had rallied, recovered the post, and drove the enemy back to their entrenchments.

General Hay was killed in this affair, while giving directions for the church to be defended to the last. In the centre the enemy also succeeded in driving in one of the picquets, after a sharp resistance, compelling the other picquets of the Second Brigade to fall back, by which the left rear of the First Brigade became exposed to the enemy's attacks. Stopford was wounded, whereupon the command of the Second Guards Brigade devolved upon Colonel Guise. Maitland's Brigade of the First Guards, as before described, was on the British right, and there the attack had not been so vigorous.

The picquets fell back upon their supports, and Lieutenant-Colonel Townshend, First Guards while bringing up his company to their assistance, was taken prisoner. The enemy at once began to destroy the entrenchments, when Major-General Howard gave directions to Colonel Maitland to advance with his Brigade of First Guards to the support, and cooperate in recovering the ground between the right and St. Etienne. Maitland had formed his Brigade on the hill above the convent, in readiness to fall upon the enemy in flank, if he attempted to push on in the direction of Boucant, and to penetrate to the bridge; but when it was found that the attack was entirely directed against the lines opposite the citadel, and that the enemy had penetrated to the left rear of his picquets, he advanced with the Third Battalion First Guards, against the French in the hollow road and field, of which they had taken possession.

The night was so dark that they could only see the enemy by the flashes of their muskets. The battalion had been ordered to lie down, and, orders being sent to Lieutenant-Colonel Woodford to make a simultaneous attack with the Coldstreams, the signal was given to charge: the two battalions sprang to their feet, and, with loud shouts, dashed against the enemy, dislodged them from the hill, and reoccupied all the posts which the British had before possessed. The French did not stand to receive them, and, fearing they might be cut off, retreated. When morning dawned a most destructive fire was opened upon their retiring columns as they crossed the glacis, and they were eventually forced to seek refuge in the citadel, having lost nearly 900 men in this, the last military operation of the war. Lieut.-General Sir John Hope was, unfortunately, taken prisoner, when moving up with the reserve.

The casualties amongst the Allies were nearly as great as amongst the enemy, amounting to 150 killed, 457 wounded, and 236 missing; but the losses of the First Guards Brigade were small in proportion to those of the other brigade, being three officers wounded, three men killed, thirty-seven wounded, and fifteen missing.

There were no casualties amongst the officers of the First Battalion First Guards. The three in the Third Battalion were, Lieutenant-Colonel Townshend, severely wounded, and taken prisoner; Lieutenant and Captain J. P. Percival, and Walter Vane, both also severely wounded. There were, altogether, sixteen casualties amongst the Guards officers, and 490 amongst their men and no less than nine officers of the Guards subsequently died of the wounds they received: an unnecessary loss, for the news of the abdication of Napoleon had been received the day before, and a suspension of hostilities had been expected that Sunday.

★★

Among the many officers of the Guards who were taken prisoners in the unfortunate sortie from Bayonne, was the Hon. H. Townshend, commonly called Bull Townshend. He was celebrated as a *bon vivant*, and in consequence of his too great indulgence in the pleasures of the table, had become very unwieldy, and could not move quick enough to please his nimble captors, so he received many prods in the back from a sharp bayonet. After repeated threats, however, he was dismissed with what our American friends would be pleased to

SORTIE FROM BAYONNE

designate "a severe booting."

The late Sir Willoughby Cotton was also a prisoner. It really seemed as if the enemy had made choice of our fattest officers. Sir Willoughby escaped by giving up his watch and all the money which he had in his pockets; but this consisting of a Spanish dollar only, the smallness of the sum subjected him to the same ignominious treatment as had been experienced by Townshend.

★★

The official news of the abdication of the emperor did not reach the camp of the Allies till the 18th of April, when it was at once communicated to the governor of the fortress; a convention was agreed upon between Wellington and Marshal Soult, for the suspension of hostilities, and at mid-day on the 20th, the Allies in front of Bayonne, hoisted the Bourbon standard, saluting it with twenty-one guns. The French garrison of Bayonne hoisted the tri-colour, and fired two shells, which was the only indication of hostility that they showed.

On the 27th an *aide-de-camp* from Soult arrived with the official intelligence of the suspension of hostilities, upon which an armistice was signed, and on the following day the white flag was displayed from the fortress, and saluted by the French, the Allied Army, then under arms, echoing back the salute.

The Brigades of Guards still remained encamped for above six weeks in the vicinity of the citadel. Peace was signed at Paris on the 30th of May; the official account of its signature reached Bayonne on the 9th of June; three days after which, on the 12th, salutes were fired by the governor at daybreak, at mid-day, and at sunset, in celebration of the event.

Orders were at the same time received for the First Brigade of Guards to march to Bordeaux, whence they were to embark for England. In accordance with these orders, they broke up their camp on the 16th of June, and, marching through the country of the Landes, arrived, on the 21st, at Bellevue. On the following day they entered Bordeaux by the "Hospital Militaire," passing by the Palais Royal and cathedral. Here the brigade remained for a month.

****

Before we left the neighbourhood of Bayonne for Bordeaux, a soldier was hanged for robbery on the sands of the Adour. This sort of punishment astonished the French almost as much as it did the soldier. On a march we were very severe; and if any of our men were caught committing an act of violence or brigandage, the offender was tried by a drum-head court martial, and hanged in a very short time.

When we reached Bordeaux, which had now become a stronghold of the Royalists, we were received by the inhabitants with a welcome which resembled what would be shown to friends and deliverers, rather than to a foreign soldiery. Nothing could be more gratifying and more acceptable to our feelings, since it was the first time after our arrival on the Continent that we met with cordiality and an apparent desire to make our quarters as comfortable as possible. The Duc d'Angoulême had reached Bordeaux before us, and no doubt his presence had prepared the way for all the friends of the Bourbons. Everywhere some description of white rag was doing duty for a Royalist banner.

I lived at M. Devignés, a rich wine merchant, who had a family of two sons and two beautiful daughters; the latter, as I thought, taken remarkable care of by their maternal parent. Here I had evidently fallen upon my legs, for not only was the family a most agreeable one, but their hospitality was of the most generous kind. Sir Stapleton Cotton was our frequent visitor, together with M. Martignac, afterward minister of Charles the Tenth.

Here I had an opportunity of meeting some of the prettiest women of a city famed all over Europe for its female beauty. The young ladies were remarkable for their taste in dress, which in those days consisted of a mantilla *à l'Espagnole*, and silken shawls of varied hues, so admirably blended that the eye was charmed with their richness of colour. The *grisettes*, who were as much admired by the soldiers as were the high dames by the officers, were remarkable for a *coquettish* species of apron of a red dye, which was only to be obtained from the neighbourhood.

Of course, we were all very anxious to taste the Bordeaux wines, but our palates, accustomed to the stronger vintages of Spain, I suspect were not in a condition to appreciate the more delicate and refined bouquets which ought to characterise claret. A *vin ordinaire*, which now at a restaurateur's would cost three *francs*, was then furnished at the hotels for fifteen *sous*; a *Larose, Lafitte, Margaux*, such as we are now paying eight or ten *francs* a bottle for, did not cost a third. I must not, however, forget that greater attention and care is now employed in the preparation of French wines. The exportation to England of the light red wines of France was not sufficiently profitable, as I learnt from my host, at that time to attract the cupidity of commerce.

In the Guards, Bordeaux was more affectionately remembered in connection with its women than its wine. We left it with regret, and the more youthful and imaginative amongst us said that we were wafted across the Channel by the gentle sighs of "the girls we left behind us."

★★★

On the 23rd of July, the First and Third Battalions, embarking in large boats, descended the river to the mouth of the Gironde, where H.M.S. *Tigre, Belle Poule,* and *Freya,* frigates, were ready to receive them. These ships sailed on the 26th and 27th of July, reaching Portsmouth at the beginning of August, when the troops being landed, the two battalions of First Guards marched to London, arriving there on the 9th and 10th August respectively.

The Waterloo Campaign: 1815

During the latter part of 1814 and the first few months of the following year, while the many and conflicting interests of the several European states were being discussed at the Congress of Vienna, the whole of Europe remained in a state of armed peace; during which, besides the Dutch and Belgians, a body of British troops, under Sir Henry Clinton, including the three second battalions of Guards, under Major-General G. Cooke, late of the First Regiment, together with some Hanoverians, continued to occupy Belgium under the terms of the Convention.

Upon the return to England of the First and Third Battalions First Guards from the south of France, on the 9th of August of this year, they received their share of recruits from the home companies, and the four companies of the Second Battalion that had been left in England were ordered to join the headquarters of their battalion in the Low Countries. The draft for the Second Battalion of the Regiment, amounting to 460 men, embarked before the end of the month, and, on arrival, in the beginning of September, at Brussels, to which town the Headquarters of the Second Battalion, as well as of the rest of the brigade, had been removed from Antwerp in July, the 2nd Battalion was raised to its proper complement, and Lord Proby, who had been removed from the Guards by the operation of the Brevet, was succeeded in the command by Colonel H. Askew. At the same time about 200 invalids and others of the First Guards were drafted out of the service companies to return to England.

The several Battalions of Guards were now mostly quartered in the St. Elizabeth and other barracks in Brussels, while some

were billeted on the inhabitants. Though the Duke of Wellington was at this time in Flanders making an inspection of the
Flemish fortresses, all the troops in the Low Countries, British as
well as foreign, were under H.R.H. the Prince of Orange, who,
on assuming, on the 18th of August, the duties of his post, appointed, amongst others, two officers of the First Guards, Captain Hon. A. de Ros and Viscount Bury, to be his *aides-de-camp.*

Nothing of particular interest occurred at Brussels during the
first months of this year; the usual parade and *feu-de-joie* took
place on the occasion of the queen's birthday, on the 18th of
January; the several garrisons of Brussels, Antwerp, Ghent, and
Mons were assembled in their respective towns on the 1st of
February, to fire a *feu-de-joie* in commemoration of the entry of
the allied troops into the capital of the country; and on the 26th
of February the Brigade of Guards, commanded on the occasion
by Colonel Henry Askew, of the First Regiment, took part in a
review of all the troops in Brussels, held on the occasion of the
Prince of Orange being raised to the Royal dignity, as sovereign
of the united countries of Holland and Belgium.

On that day Napoleon had slipped his shackles on Elba, and
landed near Cannes with 1,200 men, who were soon to be increased to a large army. All the allied sovereigns united their
armies once more, to be finally done with him. The Duke of
Wellington was at the time at Vienna, where he had gone to re-
place Lord Castlereagh as one of the representatives in Congress
of the eight European sovereigns, and, on the 13th of March, he,
in conjunction with his colleagues declared that Napoleon had
placed himself in the position of outlaw and that they would
be ready to give every assistance to France to restore peace and
make common cause against the offender.

Meanwhile the former emperor was advancing in triumph
through France, passing Grenoble, Lyons, Mâcon, Chalons, and
Auxerre. Everywhere the peasantry received him with enthusiasm and the ranks of his army daily increased. On the 20th of
March he reached Fontainebleau, where he heard that the king
had quitted Paris and fled to Belgium, and so the same evening

GENERAL ROWLAND HILL

LIEUTENANT-GENERAL SIR
THOMAS PICTON

GENERAL SIR PEREGRINE
MAITLAND

SIR WILLIAM MAYNARD
GOMM

saw Napoleon reinstalled in the Tuileries. While he was still advancing on Paris, the allied generals were assembling their forces on a line, of which the left was near Basle, on the Upper Rhine, and the right, of which the British formed a part, was near the frontier of Belgium, towards Ath and Oudenarde.

The 2nd battalion First Guards, still at Brussels, under Colonel Askew, received orders, on the 17th of March to take the field with the rest of the army; and the heavy baggage, which had been allowed while the troops were in cantonments, was sent off to Ostend. The Guards were ready to march towards the frontier on the 22nd, but a further delay of three days occurred before they were ordered to move, their destination being Enghien, thirty miles south-west of the Capital. At five in the morning of the 25th the two battalions of the First and Third Guards assembled on the Grande Place, opposite the Hotel de Ville, and were soon on the march to Hal, the battalion of Coldstreams joining a few hours later, after being relieved from the public duties.

The Prince of Orange had rashly decided to besiege Lille; and the Guards, while on their march to Enghien, received orders to continue their route twelve miles further through Enghien to Ath, which they reached on the 26th, thus strengthening the extreme right of the allied line, and being in a position to resist any attack from the direction of Valenciennes. Towards the end of March, previous to the Duke of Wellington taking command of the king's forces on the continent, the British troops in Belgium amounted to 7,300 cavalry and 18,000 infantry, the Hanoverians to 14,000 men.

The three battalions of Guards still formed at this period only one brigade, making part of the first division strength being:—1st Regiment, 974; Coldstreams, 765; 3rd Regiment, 883 men. A Light Division was also formed, consisting of Sir Henry Clinton's Brigade, Adams's 52nd and 95th Regiments, and a brigade of the King's German Legion, the Guards were held ready at Ath, to move forward on Lille at the shortest notice, having always one day's provisions ready cooked with them;

but, in consequence of the return of Napoleon to Paris, and the movements of the Imperial forces,(together no doubt with the intercession of wiser minds and firmer hands) the project of besieging Lille was abandoned, and the brigade returned, on the 4th of April, to Enghien and its neighbourhood, where it remained until hostilities began.

The British Government resolved to increase the number of the king's troops in the Low Countries. Many regiments already in England were armed for this service, and those returning from America were, on their arrival, at once sent on to Belgium. Of the Guards, the 3rd Battalion of the First Regiment, under Colonel Hon. William Stuart, was eventually selected to join the 2nd Battalion abroad, being ordered, on the 2nd of April, to prepare for immediate service, and it marched from the Birdcage Walk, at six a.m. on Wednesday, the 5th of April, to Deptford, for embarkation.

On the 1st of April, it was first decided to send another battalion of the First Guards to join the Second in Flanders, the First Battalion was put in orders, and warned for that duty, to proceed to Deal on the following Tuesday, the 4th; but on the 2nd of the month, when fully prepared to start, it was countermanded, and the Third Battalion ordered to proceed in its stead. From Deptford the 3rd Battalion marched to Ramsgate, arriving there on the 9th of April, when it immediately embarked, and reached Ostend on the following day; on the 11th it proceeded by canal to Bruges, and on the 12th to Ghent by the same means of transport, reaching the village of Marcq, near Enghien.

The Duke of Wellington assumed the command of the King's British and Hanoverian forces on the Continent on the 11th of April. Major-Generals George Cooke and Peregrine Maitland were originally, on the 15th of April, named to command the two brigades into which the four battalions were to be divided on the 3rd Battalion First Guards reaching its destination; but on its arrival at Enghien Major-General Cooke was at once put in command of the whole of the First Division of the army composed of the above two Brigades of Guards.

The First Brigade was composed of the Second and Third Battalions First Guards, each above 1,000 strong, under the command of Major-General Peregrine Maitland; the second of the two battalions of the Second and Third Regiments, also above 1,000 strong each, under Major-General Sir John Byng. But until the arrival of this latter officer, Colonel Hepburn, commanding Second Battalion Third Guards was left in temporary command of the Second Brigade.

With the view to consolidating and amalgamating the two armies of Great Britain and Hanover with those of Holland and Belgium, the infantry and artillery of all these countries were divided into two great army corps, as follows:—The First, composed of the 1st and 3rd Divisions of Dutch-Hanoverians, and of the 2nd and 3rd Divisions of the Dutch-Belgic Army, was put under the orders of the Prince of Orange; and the Second, composed of the 2nd Divisions of the British and Hanoverians, and of the 1st Division of the Dutch-Belgic Army, was put under Lord Hill, who was also appointed second in command. Thus, the British Guards were again placed under the directions of the Prince of Orange. The Allied Army assembled at Waterloo amounted to near 70,000 men, of which 25,400 men were British, 17,700 German Legion and Hanoverians, 6,000 Brunswickers, 3,000 Nassauers, and 17,500 Dutch-Belgic.

During their stay near Enghien the several battalions of Guards were quartered partly in the town itself and partly in the adjacent villages, such as Marcq, and Hove on the road to Nivelles, being frequently exercised and marched out in divisions and brigades; and, as we shall soon see, their marching powers were put to a severe test on the first day of the ensuing campaign. Reviews of cavalry and infantry, balls at Brussels, and cricket matches now filled up the time.

On the 30th of May the whole division marched into cantonments for the purpose of being reviewed on the following day by the Prince of Orange, at Bruyère de Corteau, near the high road leading from Soignies to Mons. This also was a trying day, for the troops marched at two in the morning, and though the weather was bad, they had gone over forty miles before their return in the evening.

★★

Two battalions of my regiment had started from Brussels; the other (the second), to which I belonged, remained in London, and I saw no prospect of taking part in the great events which were about to take place on the Continent. Early in June I had the honour of dining with Colonel Darling, the deputy adjutant-general, and I was there introduced to Sir Thomas Picton, as a countryman and neighbour of his brother, Mr. Turberville, of Evenney Abbey, in Glamorganshire.

He was very gracious, and, on his two *aides-de-camp*—Major Tyler and my friend Chambers, of the Guards—lamenting that I was obliged to remain at home, Sir Thomas said, "Is the lad really anxious to go out?" Chambers answered that it was the height of my ambition. Sir Thomas inquired if all the appointments to his staff were filled up; and then added, with a grim smile, "If Tyler is killed, which is not at all unlikely, I do not know why I should not take my young countryman; he may go over with me if he can get leave." I was overjoyed at this, and, after thanking the general a thousand times, made my bow and retired.

I was much elated at the thoughts of being Picton's *aide-de-camp,* though that somewhat remote contingency depended upon my friends Tyler, or Chambers, or others, meeting with an untimely end; but at eighteen *on ne doute de rien.* So, I set about thinking how I should manage to get my outfit, in order to appear at Brussels in a manner worthy of the *aide-de-camp* of the great general. As my funds were at a low ebb, I went to Cox and Greenwood's, those staunch friends of the hard-up soldier. Sailors may talk of the "little cherub that sits up aloft," but commend me, for liberality, kindness, and generosity, to my old friends in Craig's Court. I there obtained two hundred pounds, which I took with me to a gambling-house in St. James's Square, where I managed, by some wonderful accident, to win six hundred pounds; and, having thus obtained the sinews of war, I made numerous purchases, amongst others two first-rate horses at Tattersall's for a high figure, which were embarked for Ostend, along with my groom. I had not got leave; but I thought I should get back, after the great battle that appeared imminent, in time to mount guard at St. James's.

On a Saturday I accompanied Chambers in his carriage to Ramsgate, where Sir Thomas Picton and Tyler had already arrived. During my passage to Ostend, with Sir Thomas Picton, *en route* to Waterloo, the general, whose demeanour was stern and rather forbidding, and of whom we all stood very much in awe, was on this occasion in great good humour and high spirits. He talked, with his usual oaths (which the reader will pardon me if I transcribe), a good deal about the Peninsular War, and the relative merits of the English and French armies. He greatly praised the soldier-like qualities and military talents of the French officers, and said:

"If I had fifty thousand such men as I commanded in Spain, with French officers at their head, I'm d——d if I wouldn't march from one end of Europe to the other."

We were all astounded at this praise of the French; and Chambers, very much piqued, observed:

"This is the first time we have heard, Sir Thomas, that French officers were superior to ours."

"What!" said Picton, "never heard they were superior to ours? Why, d—n it, where is our military education? where our military schools and colleges? We have none: absolutely none. Our greatest generals, Marlborough and Wellington, learnt the art of war in France. Nine French officers out of ten can command an army, whilst our fellows, though as brave as lions, are totally and utterly ignorant of their profession. D—n it, sir, they know nothing. We are saved by our non-commissioned officers, who are the best in the world."

We all felt very much disgusted and humiliated at these remarks, and considered them at the time very unjust; but I am now certain that the general was right, and that our officers at that time, beyond extraordinary dash and pluck, had none of the qualities required in those who were destined to command the finest troops in the world.

That true soldier, General Foy, in his history of the Peninsular War, is of the same opinion as the gallant Picton respecting our commissioned and non-commissioned officers; and he had many good opportunities of judging, for he was opposed to us on many a hard-fought field: but now, thank Heaven, our system is much improved. Patronage can no longer do everything, and a strict examination is necessary for all candidates for commissions in the army.

We remained in port for the Sunday, and embarked on Monday in a vessel which had been hired for the general and suite. On the same day we arrived at Ostend, and put up at a hotel in the square, where I was surprised to hear the general, in excellent French, get up a flirtation with our very pretty waiting-maid.

Sir Thomas Picton was a strong-built man, about the middle height, and considered very like the Hetman Platoff. He generally wore a blue frock coat, very tightly buttoned up to the throat; a very large black silk neckcloth, showing little or no shirt-collar; dark trousers, boots, and a round hat: it was in this very dress that he was attired at Quatre Bras, as he had hurried off to the scene of action before his uniform arrived.

After sleeping at Ostend, the general and Tyler went the next morning to Ghent, and on Thursday to Brussels. I proceeded by boat to Ghent, and, without stopping, hired a carriage, and arrived in time to order rooms for Sir Thomas at the Hôtel d'Angleterre, Rue de la Madeleine, at Brussels. Our horses followed us.

While we were at breakfast, Colonel Canning came to inform the general that the Duke of Wellington wished to see him immediately. Sir Thomas lost not a moment in obeying the order of his chief, leaving the breakfast-table and proceeding to the park, where Wellington was walking with Fitzroy

Somerset and the Duke of Richmond.

Picton's manner was always more familiar than the duke liked in his lieutenants, and on this occasion, he approached him in a careless sort of way, just as he might have met an equal. The duke bowed coldly to him and said, "I am glad you are come, Sir Thomas; the sooner you get on horseback the better: no time is to be lost. You will take the command of the troops in advance. The Prince of Orange knows by this time that you will go to his assistance." Picton appeared not to like the duke's manner; for when he bowed and left, he muttered a few words, which convinced those who were with him that he was not much pleased with his interview.

★★

During the first fortnight of June, while little alteration was made in the disposition of the Allied Army, Wellington was watching for the first movements of the enemy, which was assembling its forces at Beaumont. In the early part of the month, Napoleon had been directing from Paris the movements of his troops on the Belgian frontier. His first corps was at Valenciennes, opposite Ath, where the extreme right of the British Army, under Lord Hill, was posted. His second at Maubeuge, in a position to threaten the centre of the Anglo-Hanoverian and Belgic Army, while others were assembling along the frontier further south opposite the Prussians.

The French Imperial Guard left Paris at the beginning of June, and on the 13th the whole of the French troops were concentrating at Beaumont, south of the Sambre, opposite to the Prussian Army under Blücher, who was in position in front of Charleroi.

Napoleon, having quitted Paris on the 12th reached Beaumont on the 14th of June, when he issued his last address to his army, and putting his troops in motion, he promptly crossed the Sambre on the morning of the 15th, and attacked the Prussians, who retired through Charleroi and Fleurus to a position near Ligny.

Wellington was apprised of these movements; and the information of the passage of the river by Napoleon, and of his attack upon the Prussians, was brought to Enghien by a dragoon about two o'clock on the same afternoon. At that time the Second Battalion First Guards was quartered in the town, the right wing of the Third Battalion at Marcq, the left wing at the village of Hove, and upon the arrival of further information at eight o'clock in the evening of the 15th, that the Prussians were retiring, the right wing of the Third Battalion was directed to join the left wing at Hove, and remain with it till further orders.

On the morning of the 15th, the duke had given directions for the 1st Division to assemble at Ath, but when, at a late hour of that day, the news of the French advance reached Brussels, he issued an order dated ten o'clock at night, directing, amongst other things, that the 1st Division should move from Enghien to Braine le Comte. This order reached Enghien at half-past one in the morning of the 16th. The drums immediately beat to arms, and at two, the Guards having assembled at Hove, were ready to move off. At four o'clock they commenced their march, the First Brigade leading, preceded by its light companies under Lord Saltoun. Their route led them over the old battlefield of Steinkirk, and they reached Braine le Comte at nine in the morning, having been joined on the march by the second brigade under Byng.

The first division, after experiencing some delay in marching through this town owing to its crowded state, halted for a few hours on its eastern side, while General Cooke, commanding the division, made a reconnaissance to the southward. On his return at mid-day, he took upon himself the responsibility of continuing the march of the division towards Nivelles, ten miles further on, though the heat of the day was excessive, and the men were suffering from the weight of their packs. The division of Guards were therefore again *en route*, and in due course arrived at three o'clock at a position within half-a-mile of Nivelles, where they expected to rest from their day's march, but they had not halted many minutes and piled arms, before an *aide-de-camp* brought an order to advance immediately.

The division was again under arms, and as it was supposed from the firing having become heavy, and apparently very close, that the enemy was entering Nivelles on the other side, it moved off at the double down the hill to encounter them. After passing through the town unopposed, the march was continued to Hautain Caroll, where the artillery was allowed to pass to the front along the *chaussée* leading to Namur. During this part of the march many wounded were passed going to the rear, and a wounded officer of the 44th Regiment among them urged the quick advance of the division, as things he said, 'were going on badly' for the Allies. As the march continued, more and more wounded were met on the roadside, telling of the seriousness of the work going on in front.

At about five o'clock in the afternoon, the leading companies of the First Guards, *viz.*, the Light Infantry under Lord Saltoun, arrived at a critical moment at the north-western extremity of a wood called the Bois de Bossu, about three-quarters of a mile long and 300 yards broad, which lay to their right on the south side of the *chaussée*, near Quatre Bras. The French had just taken possession of this wood, thereby seriously threatening the duke's communication with the Prussians. It appears that Napoleon, quickly following up the previous day's passage of the Sambre, had, about two o'clock on the 16th, attacked with Ney's *corps d'armée* the left of the Dutch-Belgian Army under the Prince of Orange, that was in position in front of Quatre Bras, while he engaged the Prussians at Ligny

On the first information of the direction of Ney's advance, Wellington had ordered the whole British Army to move to its left on those cross roads. The 5th division under Picton, at Brussels, being despatched at once to the threatened point, passed by Genappes, and was for some hours, until the arrival of the First Division of Guards, the only corps of British troops that came to the assistance of the Prince of Orange.

★★

I got upon the best of my two horses, and followed Sir

Thomas Picton and his staff to Quatre Bras at full speed. His division was already engaged in supporting the Prince of Orange, and had deployed itself in two lines in front of the road to Sombref when he arrived. Sir Thomas immediately took the command. Shortly afterward, Kempt's and Pack's brigades arrived by the Brussels road, and part of Alten's division by the Nivelles road.

Ney was very strong in cavalry, and our men were constantly formed into squares to receive them. The famous Kellerman, the hero of Marengo, tried a last charge, and was very nearly being taken or killed, as his horse was shot under him when very near us. Wellington at last took the offensive; a charge was made against the French, which succeeded, and we remained masters of the field. I acted as a mere spectator, and got, on one occasion, just within twenty or thirty yards of some of the *cuirassiers*; but my horse was too quick for them.

★★

A sharply-contested action raged during the whole afternoon as the several regiments of the 5th Division, the troops under the Duke of Brunswick, and the contingent of Nassau, successively reached the scene of action. The French, superior in infantry, and possessing more than double the force of cavalry, made repeated attacks upon the hard-pressed lines of the Allies. Eventually, the French light troops succeeded in driving the Dutch–Belgian infantry out of the Bois de Bossu, while some of them almost cleared the space between that wood and the high road. Picton's 5th Division was already very much reduced, and it had become not only impracticable to attack, but it was doubtful that that the Allies were even maintaining their own ground. At this critical time the the leading Brigade of Guards, after a march of twenty-six miles, changed the aspect of affairs and caused the French skirmishers to falter.

The Prince of Orange, who had galloped along the road to meet the British Guards, ordered the light companies of the First Regiment, under Lord Saltoun, to advance into the wood to the right of the road, and drive the enemy out of it. Lord Saltoun not perceiving the enemy at the moment, as they were mostly concealed from view, asked the prince where they were? The prince, mistaking this for hesitation on the part of the officer, replied, in a hurried, hasty manner, "Sir, if you don't like to undertake it, I'll find someone."

Saltoun quietly repeated his question; and on its being pointed out to him that they were in the wood, formed his line of skirmishers, and led the attack. A small stream runs north and south, through the centre of this wood, and at its eastern extremity, furthest from where the Guards approached, is a hollow way, affording protection to troops who may occupy it. As the leading battalion companies of the Second Battalion, under Colonel Askew, came up, they also were ordered by the prince to enter the wood, two companies at a time, and, though wearied with a fifteen hours' march, the men received the order with a cheer, and, with fixed bayonets, pushed forward after their comrades.

Once in the wood, the leading companies had nothing to guide them but the sound of the enemy's firing. The enemy made a resolute defence, they were driven back on every side, and the loud sharp rattle of musketry, which was heard gradually but steadily advancing indicated the progress of the British Guards. The French skirmishers attempted to take advantage of the rivulet, which crosses the wood, to form up, and halt the further progress of the attack; but their stand was only momentary, for the First Guards, forcing their way across, charged, and, with a cheer, drove everything before them, until they emerged on the other side.

During this manoeuvre, the Light Companies sustained some additional loss from the hasty and hurried manner in which the battalion companies were ordered forward by the Prince of Orange, to support Lord Saltoun, for, upon entering the wood, and hearing a heavy fire in their front, these imagined it was the enemy, and commenced firing, and although Saltoun's subaltern, Charles Ellis, was sent back to explain, it was impossible to stop the firing till they emerged wood, at the other end.

LIGNY and QUATRE BRAS
Scale, 1:119,000

From the spot where the Guards came into the open, they observed the 33rd Regiment lying sheltered, behind a low hedge, about 150 yards to their left rear, while on their right was the deep ravine or hollow way before referred to, and the Guards had no sooner reached this spot than they became exposed to the direct fire of the enemy's artillery and reserve infantry. The thickness of the undergrowth had thrown the line into some confusion; and as it continued to be exposed to this galling fire of artillery, to which no return could be made, it was deemed advisable to draw back to the stream in the wood, which was more out of range; but even here, under the comparative shelter of the trees, some men were killed or maimed by the artillery fire that the French continued to direct upon them.

The Third Battalion of the First Guards, under Colonel Stuart, had now come up, and the regiment, after a few moments' rest, again advanced, being ordered to form line outside, and to the left, of the wood. As the companies had got mixed in advancing through the tangled thicket, the men formed up in succession to the right as they came into the open; and men of other regiments who had been engaged before the First Division arrived, gallantly left its cover and fell in, taking the opportunity of renewing the fight with the Guards. Their right now rested on the trees, while their left extended through the fields of standing corn, towards the *chaussée*, leading from Brussels to Charleroi.

In this formation General Maitland again and again led forward the First Guards to the attack, and as frequently drove the enemy back, but could never get beyond a certain point. The commanding officers of both battalions, Askew and Stuart, were wounded and put *hors de combat* in these repeated encounters, and were succeeded by Colonels Edward Stables and Francis D'Oyly. Though the Guards could not break the enemy's line, they stood steadily pouring a withering fire into the French columns, as these attempted gradually to deploy; while the French Cavalry continually moved about, seeking for an opportunity to charge.

When the brigade had emerged from the wood to form line, a battalion of Brunswickers followed it into the open, and was in the act of moving, so as to form up on the Guards' left, when the French cavalry came suddenly down on the left flank of the Second Battalion, forcing it bark towards the wood; and it being impossible to form square in presence of the enemy, owing to the previous irregular formation of the line, the men intuitively made for the protection offered to them by the hollow way. Here the line was immediately reformed, protected from any further cavalry attacks, and again the men commenced pouring upon their assailants a fire so destructive as nearly to annihilate them. Nothing perhaps could have better tested the perfect discipline of these battalions of Guards than the speed with which, after having been temporarily in confusion by a sudden charge of cavalry, they rallied re-formed, and, becoming themselves the assailants, repelled the enemy.

The Brunswickers, whose front became exposed when the Guards were forced into the wood formed square, and, opening fire upon the advancing cavalry, materially assisted in their destruction. Many Frenchmen were here taken prisoners, and several of their horses which fled riderless were appropriated as fresh chargers by the field officers of the Guards. The firing was kept up as long as daylight lasted, when General Maitland led the Third Battalion forward beyond the outskirts of the wood, for which the enemy no longer contended, and throwing out a line of picquets in his front for the night, showing thereby undisputed possession of the battlefield, he directed Colonel Stables, who brought the Second Battalion out of action, to move his men to the *chaussée*, at the end of the wood, where they enjoyed a well-merited short rest before the labours of another day commenced.

The losses of the two battalions, First Guards, at Quatre Bras, were, very severe. In the Second Battalion there were 3 officers, 1 sergeant, 22 rank and file killed; 4 officers, 6 sergeants, 250 rank and file wounded. In the Third Battalion 3 officers, 2 sergeants, 1 drummer, 17 rank and file killed; 4 officers, 9 sergeants,

Cavalry attack on the squares at Waterloo

1 drummer, and 225 rank and file wounded. Total casualties, 6 officers killed, 8 wounded; 43 men killed, 491 wounded: in all 548 casualties. The officers of the First Guards killed were buried the following morning by a party of their regiment under a large tree on the right of the wood nearest towards Nivelles. One of them, shot down in one of the last attacks by a French cavalry skirmisher was young Lord James Hay, who had recently celebrated his eighteenth birthday.

★★★

The recent (at time of original publication) works of M. Theirs and Colonel Charras, Quinet's defence of Marshal Ney, and Victor Hugo's romance of *Les Miserables*, have directed public attention with renewed interest to the Battle of Waterloo, and the various episodes connected with it.

I have therefore ventured, to add a few further reminiscences of that eventful day. Though I took but a humble part in this great contest, yet I had opportunities of seeing and hearing much. My anecdotes are derived either from personal experiences during and after the battle. They are derived either from personal experience and observation, from the conversation of those to whom they refer, or from the common talk of the army at the time; and many of these anecdotes may be new to my readers.

But before I begin to retrace those scenes and episodes (which I fear will be in a very imperfect and desultory manner) I must state that, while my admiration for the great duke and my gallant comrades is unbounded, yet I repudiate any share in the vulgar John Bull exultation which glories in having "licked the confounded French."

Though I cannot agree with their writers in attributing their defeat to ill luck, yet I am willing to admit that the tide of success had turned against Napoleon, that he was not altogether what he had been, when at Austerlitz and Wagram he carried all before him. Then, flushed with victory, he was animated with the certainty of success, which in itself was an earnest of triumph. But all was changed when the mighty conqueror came to play his last stake on the field of Waterloo. He knew defeat was possible, for he had been vanquished; and, though his prestige was immense, yet the *Garde Imperiale*, and the other veterans of his noble army, who in former days had only thought of victory when commanded by him, now whispered together of dying with him.

Even the bravest of soldiers, or the most desperate of gamblers, plays his last stake with some degree of emotion and hesitation, knowing that all depends on the throw; and Napoleon, feeling that (humanly speaking) he held in his hand the fate of empires, and his own, knew that if he lost the day, all was over with him in this world. He was then not quite his former self; and he certainly committed several errors about the middle of the day, and showed considerable hesitation as to the orders to be given. The chief mistake he made, in my humble opinion, was this: he did not support the brilliant charges of his cavalry, and the tremendous fire of his numerous and well-served artillery, by the general advance of his infantry, until it was too late and his cavalry were annihilated.

★★★

The French were not prepared to renew the contest on the following morning. Ney had retired on the road to Frasne, three miles to the rear; and as far as the British troops were concerned, Wellington could have made his dispositions to follow up the enemy, but, as Blücher had on the previous evening been obliged to relinquish his position and retire upon Wavre, after the action at Ligny, where he maintained himself during the whole day against the repeated assaults of the French under Napoleon in person, the duke resolved upon likewise making a movement to the rear, and taking up a position in front of the Forest of Soignies, keeping up the communication on his left with Blücher,

The army that had been at Quatre Bras had to cross the narrow bridge spanning the River Dyle at Genappes, on the road to

Brussels; and to cover this operation he left a strong rear-guard on the heights above Quatre Bras, to deceive the enemy as to the strength of the British Army remaining in his front. When Napoleon had completed his dispositions with the view to re-newing the attack, he found only a rear-guard of cavalry op-posed to him, which then began to leisurely retire. The French cavalry were sent in instant pursuit, and overtook the British light cavalry at Genappes. Lord Uxbridge brought forward the Life Guards, and effectually checked the pursuit, thus allow-ing the British Army to take up their position before Waterloo without further molestation.

Upon the order being given for the Allied Army to retire from the neighbourhood of Quatre Bras, the First Division of Guards left their ground a little after eleven o'clock, and moved along the *chaussée* leading to Brussels. The day was excessively hot, with indications of a coming storm. The roads were much crowded, but the movement continued with little interruption, and the stoppages were but short, except on one occasion at Genappes, caused by the narrowness of the bridge at that place over the Dyle.

After a march of about eight miles the First Division quitted the high road, and moved to its left along a cart track that soon brought it behind the *château* and farm of Hougoumont, with its garden, orchard, and wood.

Here the division was halted, and the men were preparing their bivouac for the night, when orders came to move to the right and take up a position on the next rise along the south-west side of the *chaussée* leading from Nivelles to Mont St. Jean. Scarcely had the several battalions moved to their new position than the storm of rain that had long been threatening came down, and continued throughout the greater part of the night, soaking the men to the skin.

★★

On the 17th, Wellington retreated upon Waterloo, about eleven o'clock. The infantry were masked by the cavalry in two lines, parallel to the Namur road. Our cavalry retired on the approach of the French cavalry, in three columns, on the Brussels road. A torrent of rain fell, upon the emperor's ordering the heavy cavalry to charge us; while the fire of sixty or eighty pieces of cannon showed that we had chosen our position at Waterloo. Chambers said to me, "Now, Gronow, the loss has been very severe in the Guards, and I think you ought to go and see whether you are wanted; for, as you have really nothing to do with Picton, you had better join your regiment, or you may get into a scrape."

Taking his advice, I rode off to where the Guards were stationed. The officers—amongst whom I remember Colonel Thomas and Brigade-Major Miller—expressed their astonishment and amazement on seeing me, and exclaimed, "What the deuce brought you here? Why are you not with your battalion in London? Get off your horse, and explain how you came here!"

Things were beginning to look a little awkward, when Gunthorpe, the adjutant, a great friend of mine, took my part and said, "As he is here, let us make the most of him: there's plenty of work for everyone. Come, Gronow, you shall go with Captain Clements and a detachment to the village of Waterloo, to take charge of the French prisoners."

"What the deuce shall I do with my horse?" I asked. Upon which Captain Stopford, *aide-de-camp* to Sir John Byng, volunteered to buy him. Having thus once more become a foot-soldier, I started according to orders, and arrived at Waterloo.

Captain Clements, brother of Lord Leitrim, had charge of some hundreds of French prisoners. They had been taken at Quatre Bras, and were confined in a barn and the courtyard of a large farmhouse. As ill-luck would have it, Clements did not place sentinels on the other side of the wall, which overlooked the plain leading to the forest of Soignies; the consequence was that, with the aid of a large wagon which had been left in the yard, several of the prisoners scaled the wall, and made their escape. As soon as it was night, some more poor fellows

The Final Advance at Waterloo

attempted to follow their example; but this time the alarm was given, and our men fired, and killed or wounded a dozen of them.

This firing at so late an hour brought several officers of the staff from the neighbouring houses to ascertain the cause, and among them came my poor friend Chambers, who kindly invited me to Sir Thomas Picton's quarters to supper. I accompanied him thither, and after groping our way into the house, for it was very dark, we passed the door of a room in which Sir Thomas himself was lying. I heard him groan, from the pain of the wound he had received at Quatre Bras, but did not, of course, venture to disturb him, and we passed on into a small hall, where I got some cold meat and wine.

At daylight, on the 18th, we were agreeably surprised to see a detachment of the 3rd Guards, commanded by Captain Wigston and Ensign George Anson, the lamented general who died in India, who had been sent to relieve us. I took the opportunity of giving Anson, then a fine lad of seventeen, a silver watch, made by Barwise, which his mother, Lady Anson, had requested me to take over to him. Bob Clements and I then proceeded to join our regiment.

The road was ankle-deep in mud and slough; and we had not proceeded a quarter of a mile when we heard the trampling of horses' feet, and on looking around perceived a large cavalcade of officers coming at full speed. In a moment we recognised the duke himself at their head. He was accompanied by the Duke of Richmond, and his son, Lord William Lennox. The entire staff of the army was close at hand: the Prince of Orange, Count Pozzo di Borgo, Baron Vincent, the Spanish General Alava, Prince Castel Cicala, with their several *aides-de-camp*; Felton Harvey, Fitzroy Somerset, and Delaney were the last that appeared. They all seemed as gay and unconcerned as if they were riding to meet the hounds in some quiet English county.

★★★

About six o'clock in the evening the four Light Companies of the division were ordered to take possession of the farmhouse and grounds of Hougoumont;—the two light companies of the First Guards, under Lord Saltoun and Ellison, occupied the orchard and wood, while the two of the Second Brigade occupied the farmhouse and garden, which was surrounded by a wall. The night and the following morning were spent by the light companies in making this position as strong as their means would allow them, barricading the gates and otherwise rendering the buildings as defensible as possible, and at Saltoun's suggestion, loop-holing the garden wall.

During the first part of the night the French brought up their advanced posts close to the line of picquets of the First Guards in the wood and orchard, though without attempting to molest them; but about two in the morning, as their *tirailleurs* were advancing too near, Lieutenant-Colonel Ellison, who was picquet officer for the night, was ordered from the orchard into the wood to drive them out. This he accomplished, and the wood being an open grove without undergrowth , and easily traversed in every direction, the advanced files of the picquets could keep up the communication with each other without difficulty.

The effective strength of the British troops on the morning of the 18th June was 15,418 infantry, of which the British Guards supplied about 3,600, 5,877 cavalry, and 40,94 gunners; total 25,389 men and 78 guns. The total effective strength of the foreign contingents of the Allied Army was—King's German Legion 6,793, Hanoverians near 11,000, Brunswickers 6,300, Nassauers 2,926, and Dutch Belgians 17,488, making a total of 69,894 men and 164 guns.

The effective strength of the French Army at the same time was 70,428 men and 240 guns.

The Allied Army was in position by eight o'clock on the morning of the 18th of June, on the rising ground before Waterloo. The line extended along the front of the forest of Soignies; the extreme right, under Lord Hill, consisted of Clinton's second division, composed of Adams's brigade, *viz*. the 52nd, 71st, and

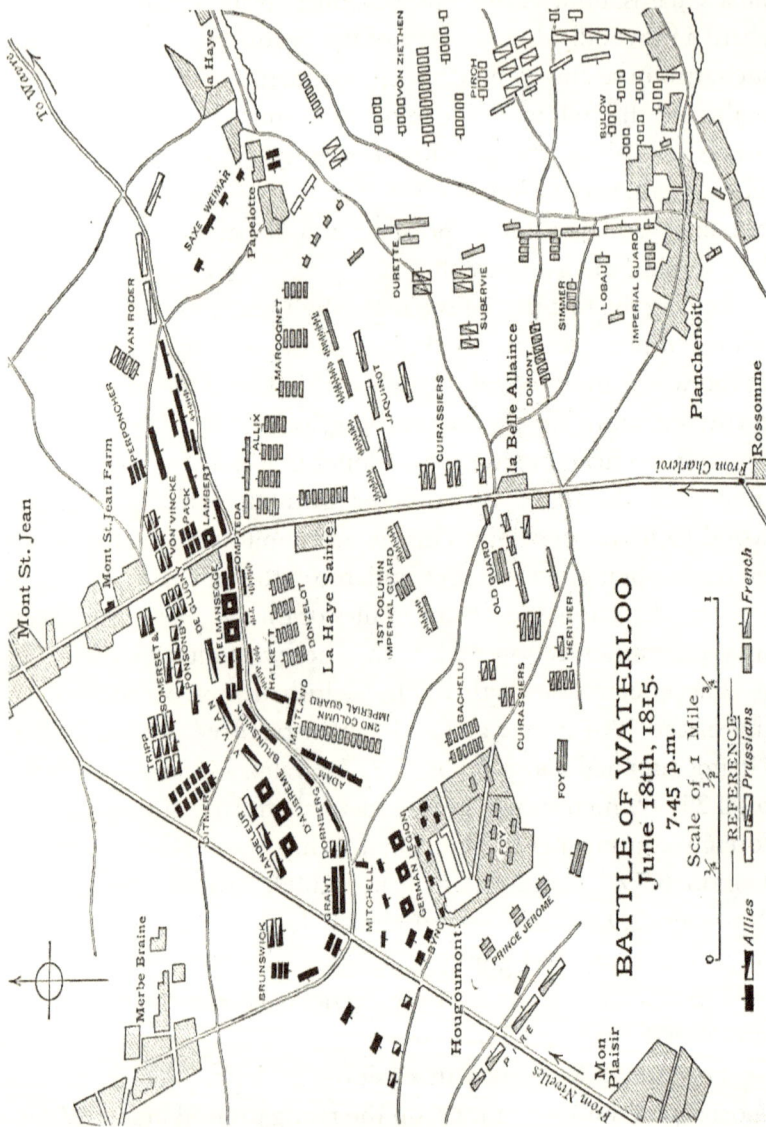

BATTLE OF WATERLOO
June 18th, 1815.
7.45 p.m.

Scale of 1 Mile

REFERENCE
Allies
Prussians
French

part of the 95th Regiments, of a brigade of the King's German Legion under Du Plat, and a Hanoverian brigade under Colonel Halkett. These were thrown back towards Merbe Braine, defending the road from Nivelles, and were prepared, either to repel an attempt to turn the right of the position, or to move up in support of the right centre, should that part of the line, as eventually proved to be the case, be the principal object of the enemy's attacks.

The left of the Allied Army rested on Ter la Hay and Papelotte, and was composed of Picton's Fifth Division of the British Army and Vandeleur's and Vivian's cavalry.

In front of the left centre of the Charleroi road was the farm of La Haye Sainte, occupied by Hanoverian battalion, while in front of the right centre was the before-mentioned *château* and farm of Hougoumont, held by the Guards and some foreign troops. This was the key of the position, and the division of Guards was formed in rear of it; the Second Brigade immediately in rear, ready to support the garrison if hard pressed; the First Brigade to the left of the Second, with its left resting on Halkett's Brigade, which, with Kielmansegge's and Ompteda's Brigades, extended towards the Charleroi road.

The several battalions of the Guards were posted on the rising ground above Hougoumont, in the following order. The Third Battalion First Guards on the extreme left, on the crest of the ridge, in quarter-distance column of companies, at deploying distance from the right of Halkett's Brigade; the Second Battalion First Guards in the same formation, was to the right rear of the Third Battalion, the reverse slope, and immediately under the crest of the hill. The Second Brigade, under Byng, stood on the crest of the ridge between the right of the First Brigade and the Nivelles road, completely commanding the *château* and grounds of Hougoumont, and thus forming a support to the troops stationed there.

★★★

In about half an hour we joined our comrades in camp, who

were endeavouring to dry their accoutrements by the morning sun, after a night of rain and discomfort in their bivouac. I was now greeted by many of my old friends (whom I had not had time to speak to the day before, when I was sent off to the village of Waterloo) with loud cries of "How are you, old fellow? Take a glass of wine and a bit of ham? it will, perhaps, be your last breakfast."

Then Burges called out, "Come here, Gronow, and tell us some London news."

He had made himself a sort of gipsy tent, with the aid of some blankets, a sergeant's halberd, and a couple of muskets. My dear old friend was sitting upon a knapsack, with Colonel Stuart (who afterward lost his arm), eating cold pie and drinking champagne, which his servant had just brought from Brussels. I was not sorry to partake of his hospitality, and, after talking together some time, we were aroused by the drums beating to arms. We fell in, and the muster-roll having been called, the piling of arms followed; but we were not allowed to leave our places.

The position taken up by the British Army was an excellent one; it was a sort of ridge, very favourable for artillery, and from which all the movements of the French could be discerned. In case of any disaster, Wellington had several roads in his rear by which a masterly retreat could have been effected through the forest on Brussels; but our glorious commander thought little about retreating; on the contrary, he set all his energies to work, and determined to win the day.

Our brigade was under the orders of General Maitland, and our division was commanded by Sir George Cooke. We occupied the right centre of the British line, and had the *château* of Hougoumont at about a quarter of a mile's distance on our right. Picton was on the extreme left at La Haye Sainte, with his division of two British and one Hanoverian brigades. Hougoumont was garrisoned by the 2nd and 3rd Regiments of the Guards, a battalion of Germans, and two battalions of artillery, who occupied the *château* and gardens. Between each regiment was a battery of guns, and nearly the whole of the cavalry was to the left of Sir Thomas Picton's division.

★★★

It had generally been understood that the Light Companies of the First Brigade of Guards under Saltoun remained permanently in the orchard and wood from the previous night till relieved in the course of the action of the 18th, Such was not the case, for in the early morning, just before dawn, a staff officer conducted to the post a battalion of Nassauers, one company of Hanoverian riflemen, and 100 Lünebergers, and handed to Lord Saltoun an order to deliver up the charge of the orchard to the officer commanding them, and to retire with his own men to join his brigade posted on the hill in rear of Hougoumont. After taking the Nassau officer over the orchard and showing him all the plans and preparations for defence, Saltoun was marching towards the First Guards' Brigade, on the ridge behind Hougoumont, when about halfway, in the early grey of the morning, he met the Duke of Wellington and Lord Fitzroy Somerset.

The duke called out, "Hallo, who are you? Where are you going?"

Saltoun immediately halted, ordered arms, directed his men to lie down, according to an invariable custom; and on advancing to the duke, explained to him the orders he had received.

The duke was surprised, and said, "Well, I was not aware of such an order; but, however, don't join the brigade yet; remain quiet here where you are until further orders from me," and then he rode away.

Saltoun remained here several hours, when, just as the battle was beginning, an *aide-de-camp* rode up and said he was to follow out his former orders and join his brigade, on reaching which, he gave up his temporary command, and resumed that of his company, in rear of his own battalion.

★★★

The day on which the Battle of Waterloo was fought

seemed to have been chosen by some providential accident for which human wisdom is unable to account. On the morning of the 18th the sun shone most gloriously, and so clear was the atmosphere that we could see the long, imposing lines of the enemy most distinctly. Immediately in front of the division to which I belonged, and, I should imagine, about half a mile from us, were posted cavalry and artillery; and to the right and left the French had already engaged us, attacking Hougoumont and La Haye Sainte. We heard incessantly the measured boom of artillery, accompanied by the incessant rattling echoes of musketry.

About half-past eleven the bands of several French regiments were distinctly heard, and soon after the French artillery opened fire. The rapid beating of the *pas de charge*, which I had often heard in Spain—and which few men, however brave they may be, can listen to without a somewhat unpleasant sensation—announced that the enemy's columns were fast approaching. On our side the most profound silence prevailed, whilst the French, on the contrary, raised loud shouts, and we heard the cry of *"Vive l'Empereur!"* from one end of their line to the other.

The battle commenced by the French throwing out clouds of skirmishers from Hougoumont to La Haye Sainte. Jerome Bonaparte's division, supported by those of Foy and Bachelu, attacked Hougoumont, the wood and garden of which were taken and retaken several times; but, after prodigies of valour performed on both sides, remained in the hands of the French, who, however, sustained immense loss, and the *château* still belonged to the invincible English Guards.

I could distinctly see the enemy advance to attack Hougoumont, when a tremendous fire of artillery was opened upon them, which had the appearance of creating some confusion and disorder in their ranks. On they went, however, and in a moment got into the orchard. Then such a fire opened on both sides, and such a smoke ensued, that, like Homer's heroes, they were hidden by a cloud, and I could see no more. I had, besides, plenty to occupy my own attention immediately afterward.

No individual officer more distinguished himself than did General Byng at the Battle of Waterloo. In the early part of the day, he was seen at Hougoumont leading his men in the thick of the fight; later he was with the battalion in square, where his presence animated to the utmost enthusiasm both officers and men. It is difficult to imagine how this courageous man passed through such innumerable dangers from shot and shell without receiving a single wound. I must also mention some other instances of courage and devotion in officers belonging to this brigade; for instance, it was Colonel Macdonell, a man of colossal stature, with Hesketh, Bowes, Tom Sowerby, and Hugh Seymour, who commanded from the inside the *château* of Hougoumont.

When the French had taken possession of the orchard, they made a rush at the principal door of the *château*, which had been turned into a fortress. Macdonell and the above officers placed themselves, accompanied by some of their men, behind the portal, and prevented the French from entering. Amongst other officers of that brigade who were most conspicuous for bravery, I would record the names of Montague, the "vigorous Gooch," as he was called, and the well-known Jack Standen.

Whilst the battle was raging in the wood and orchard, eighty French guns, mostly twelve-pounders, opened upon us, and caused a heavy loss in our ranks. At the same moment, we could perceive from our elevated position that the enemy were attacking La Haye Sainte in great force.

★★★

Lord Saltoun had no sooner re-established himself in the regimental position and ordered arms, when a shout came up, "Light infantry to the front," and "The Nassauers are driven out of the orchard"; for the French attacked, and, in spite of the fierce defence that was made, had swept them clear and clean out of it.

No time was to be lost; Saltoun was again put in command of the light companies of the First Guards, and went down the hill to attack the French. The first duty that these Light Companies had to perform that was to retake the orchard, not to resist an attack upon it; and that made a great difference in the work to be performed so far as these companies were concerned; for when they had re-occupied the wood, which they were not long in doing, they found nearly all the preparations they had made for defence completely destroyed, and during the action they had to trust to sheer hard fighting, often hand to hand, to maintain their ground.

Shortly before the action commenced, the Duke of Wellington visited the advanced position of Hougomont, occupied by the second Brigade of Guards, under Byng; and, on riding off to another part of the field, left as his parting injunctions to that general, that it was to be defended to the last extremity, and nobly were those injunctions responded to by the British Guards.

The battle commenced shortly after eleven o'clock with an attack upon this the key of the allied position by the infantry of Prince Jerome's corps, preceded by a cloud of skirmishers, while from 200 guns the French artillery opened fire along the whole line against the allied forces.

As the French skirmishers advanced upon Hougoumont they were twice checked by the direct fire of the British artillery from the rising ground above, but they eventually succeeded in effecting an entrance to the wood, and in driving back the Nassauers and Hanoverians who had occupied it, when the direct fire could no longer be continued; but the further advance of the French was soon checked by some shells from a howitzer battery, which the duke sent for, and by the return of the light companies of the First Guards, under Lord Saltoun. The companies of the Second Brigade at the same time rushed gallantly forward to relieve the foreign troops, and the four Light Companies of the two Guard's Brigades together eventually cleared the wood for a time of the French skirmishers, who retired into the fields beyond.

THE CHARGE OF LORD SALTOUN AND THE FIRST GUARDS

While Wellington had recognised this as the key of the allied position, Napoleon had also felt the necessity of securing it before he could make any impression upon the centre. Jerome's skirmishers were reinforced, and, in conjunction with General Foy's infantry on their right, renewed the attack with great vigour. The British Guards of both brigades offered a desperate resistance, retiring from tree to tree and frequently making a bold and resolute stand, but a superiority of numbers forced them at length to return to their original positions; the First Guards Light Companies on the left falling back to their position in the orchard, the Second Brigade Companies retiring to the shelter offered by the *château* itself and by a haystack standing outside.

The French skirmishers, believing all opposition to have ceased, now rapidly advanced through the wood towards the building and garden. A hedge forming the northern boundary of the wood, towards they were approaching, appeared to them to form also the enclosure of the garden beyond, and, in full confidence that they were about to become masters of it, they rushed forward *au pas de charge*: but were soon fatally undeceived; the loopholed garden wall stood thirty yards behind the hedge, running parallel to it, behind which stood the Coldstreams and Third Guards, and a deadly musketry fire bursting forth from the loopholes, suddenly brought them up surprised and staggered by so unexpected a reception, which laid low their foremost ranks. As the French could not hope to succeed in storming this little fortress by any direct attack, they had recourse to the shelter of the hedge and surrounding trees, from which they kept up for some time an unequal fire against the garrison who had so well protected themselves.

As the French battalions in support were rapidly pushed forward, the British artillery recommenced its fire upon them, causing much confusion in their ranks, of which the garrison and light companies First Guards at once took advantage, and, sallying forth from the flanks, soon regained possession of a considerable portion of the wood. On the advance of the Guards the British artillery ceased firing, whereupon the French recovering themselves and receiving further reinforcements, again advanced with such determination as to force the Guards to return, the Second Brigade to the flanks of the *château*, the First Brigade to the left of the garden wall.

The Coldstream and Guards companies, after having for some time resisted very superior forces, at length retired within the buildings, barricading the entrance gate with every available object, and manning the garden walls, so as to be prepared to resist the enemy at every point, while the companies of the First Guards retired as far as the hedge on their left of the garden wall, where Saltoun continued to maintain himself. The French in the wood finding a direct attack against the garden wall of no avail, endeavoured to come round its left flank through the orchard. Here Saltoun was prepared to meet them, and as they were passing through a gap from the wood into the orchard, he seized the opportunity, charged the head of the column with the First Guards' light Companies, and drove the enemy back into the wood.

Another attempt was shortly made by a considerable body of the enemy's light troops to turn the left flank of the grounds of Hougoumont, by advancing along the eastern hedge of the farm enclosures; while a simultaneous attack was made through the wood, and the orchard occupied by Lord Saltoun. He had already lost many men, and was once again obliged to withdraw, retiring from tree to tree till he reached the shelter of the hollow way in the rear face of the enclosure, where he awaited reinforcements before he could renew any forward movement.

The duke, from the height above, observing how matters were progressing, directed Byng to send down reinforcements from his brigade, and shortly afterwards two companies of the Third Guards were seen advancing along the eastern enclosure to meet the enemy, when Lord Saltoun, being thus reinforced on his left, and the advance of the French skirmishers in his front having exposed them to the flanking fire from the eastern garden wall, resumed the offensive, cleared the orchard of the enemy, and reoccupied its front hedge.

Lord Saltoun relates that the several attacks against the front of his post were at the time attended with more or less partial success, but that in the end the French were always repulsed; that in one of these attacks when he had been driven from the front hedge of the orchard to the hollow way in rear of it, the enemy occupied the front hedge with infantry and brought up a gun to bear upon him, which he endeavoured to seize; he failed in that attempt, but regained possession of the hedge, where he firmly established himself.

The attacks on Hougoumont were again renewed at a later hour, but they were as unavailing as the first, whereupon the French concentrated their artillery fire upon it; the duke replied with fresh British batteries, and though the fire of the enemy continued, it failed in abating either the spirit or the obstinacy of the defence. At last, the French artillery opened a fire of shells upon the post; the buildings as well as the chapel in which the wounded, both friends and foe had been placed, were soon in flames, in the midst of the which the inmates perished. But still, though the flames raged above, shells burst around, and shot ploughed through the shattered walls and windows, the British Guards held their own, and Hougoumont remained untaken.

About two o'clock, after Byng had reinforced Hougomont with two companies of the Third Guards, he perceived that these renewed attempts of the enemy upon the orchard were constantly reducing the numbers of those entrusted with its defence; acting, therefore, upon the directions given to him by the duke to relieve the men as often as he found it necessary, but to keep the post to the last moment, he desired Colonel Hepburn to move the remainder of his Second Battalion Third Guards down the slope as a further reinforcement to that position. Hepburn, on reaching the hollow way, found it occupied by very few men, viz., the survivors of the two light companies of the First Guards, under Saltoun, who (his own subaltern, Charles Ellis wounded) was left with scarcely an effective man with whom to continue the gallant defence, which he had been maintaining with varied success for nearly four hours in the wood and orchard in front of the *château*. Lord Saltoun, therefore, gave over to Hepburn the charge of that part of Hougomont, and at three o'clock rejoined his own battalion, the Third, on the heights above.

The battalion of Coldstreams, under Colonel Alexander Woodford (with the exception of two companies left on the ridge in charge of the Colours), was also subsequently sent forward to assist in the defence of Hougoumont, which a later period sustained another still more determined attack, but thanks to the opportune arrival of these comparatively fresh battalions of Guards, the enemy's efforts were as unavailing as before.

The value that Napoleon attached to the possession of this post may be estimated by the fact that eight thousand of his troops were placed *hors de combat* in these several unsuccessful attempts to carry it, and when evening and defeat came to him, the burning ruins were still in possession of its gallant defenders.

★★

At about two o'clock, Ney, with the first corps formed in four columns, advanced *en échelon*, the left wing forward. They completely defeated and put to flight a Dutch-Belgian brigade, and then attacked Picton's division. He, however, made a desperate resistance, and charged them several times, though they were four times his number. It was then that noble soldier was killed by a musket-ball. Things looked ill there; when the duke ordered up Adam's brigade, which regained the ground, and pushed eagerly forward.

Captain Chambers, of the First Guards was Picton's favourite *aide-de-camp*. In looking back to former days, I recollect with pride the friendship which existed between Chambers and myself. I owe my presence at the Battle of Waterloo to him; for by him I was introduced to Sir Thomas Picton, and as I have explained, it was by his advice that I joined my regiment the day before the battle. After Picton's death, poor Chambers, in carrying orders to Sir James Kempt to retake at all hazards the farm of La Haye Sainte, advanced at the head of the attacking column, and was in the act of receiving the sword of a French officer who had surrendered to him, when he received a musket-ball through the lungs which killed him on the spot. When the Duke of York heard of his death, H. R. H. exclaimed, "In him we have lost one of our most promising officers."

At about the same time Lord Uxbridge commanded the cavalry to charge. This order was admirably executed by Somerset on one side and by Ponsonby on the other, and was for a time completely successful. The French infantry brigades of Quiot, Donzelot, and Marcoguet were rolled up and almost annihilated; twenty guns were dismantled or spiked, and many hundred prisoners taken; several squadrons of *cuirassiers* were also charged and put to the rout. Unfortunately, our cavalry went too far without proper supports, and were charged and driven back by Milhaud's heavy cavalry and Jacquinot's lancers, and had to take refuge behind our own lines.

When Lord Uxbridge gave orders to Sir W. Ponsonby and Lord Edward Somerset to charge the enemy, our cavalry advanced with the greatest bravery, cut through everything in their way, and gallantly attacked whole regiments of infantry; but eventually they came upon a masked battery of twenty guns, which carried death and destruction through our ranks, and our poor fellows were obliged to give way. The French cavalry followed on their retreat, when, perhaps, the severest hand-to-hand cavalry fighting took place within the memory of man. The Duke of Wellington was perfectly furious that this arm had been engaged without his orders, and lost not a moment in sending them to the rear, where they remained during the rest of the day.

This disaster gave the French cavalry an opportunity of annoying and insulting us, and compelled the artillerymen to seek shelter in our squares; and if the French had been provided with tackle, or harness of any description, our guns would have been taken. It is, therefore, not to be wondered at that the duke should have expressed himself in no measured terms about the cavalry movements referred to. I recollect that,

when His Grace was in our square, our soldiers were so morti-
fied at seeing the French deliberately walking their horses between our regiment and those regiments to our right and left,
that they shouted, "Where are our cavalry? Why don't they
come and pitch into those French fellows?"

Sir William Ponsonby, after heading several splendid charges, on the retreat and on refusing to surrender, was killed by a
sergeant of a regiment of dragoons, of which I forget the number. He had got into some deep boggy ground, and was riding
a very inferior horse, which was completely blown, and whose
sluggishness cost him his life.

Lord Edward Somerset, who commanded the Household
Brigade, had a very narrow escape. His horse was killed, and
he had only just time to creep through a thick hedge and leap
on another horse before the enemy was upon him. Sir John Elley, Colonel of the Blues, and Horace Seymour, who was on the
staff, two of the most powerful men in the army, performed
deeds worthy of the *paladins* of the olden time. Horse and
man went down before them, as they swept onward in their
headlong course, and neither helmet nor cuirass could stand
against swords wielded by such strong arms.

In the charge of the Royals, Scots Greys, and Inniskillings on
the one side, and the 1st and 2nd Life Guards, Blues, and 1st
Dragoon Guards on the other, the Scots Greys and Blues were
ordered to act as supports. This their excessive ardour prevented them from doing, and they charged with the others.
On their return the want of supports was grievously felt. Colonel Ferrier of the 1st Life Guards, Lieutenant-Colonel Fitzgerald
of the 2nd Life Guards, and Colonel Fuller of the 1st Dragoon
Guards were killed; Major Packe of the Blues was killed by a
sword-thrust from a French sergeant; and Clement Hill, who
afterward commanded that regiment, received a lance-thrust
which nearly pinned him to his saddle.

Lieutenant Tathwell of the Blues was taken prisoner, and
as he was being conducted to the rear of the French Army, a
wounded French officer, who was being carried by four sol-

diers, ordered Tathwell to be brought up to him, and inflicted several kicks upon the unfortunate prisoner. Tathwell's captors seemed very much shocked at this infamous treatment, so different to the usual behaviour of the French, but did not dare to remonstrate.

Captain, afterward Colonel Kelly, of the Life Guards, of undaunted courage and very powerful frame, in the deadly encounter with the *cuirassiers* of the Imperial Guard, performed prodigies of valour.

In the gallant, and, for a time, successful charge of the Household Brigade, he greatly distinguished himself; and when our gallant fellows, after sustaining a terrible fire of artillery, were attacked by an overwhelming force of French cavalry, and were forced to retreat behind our squares, Kelly was seen cutting his way through a host of enemies. Shaw, the famous prize-fighter, a private in his regiment, came to his assistance, and these two heroes fought side by side, killing or disabling many of their antagonists, till poor Shaw, after receiving several wounds, was killed from a thrust through the body by a French colonel of *cuirassiers*, who in his turn received a blow from Kelly's sword, which cut through his helmet and stretched him lifeless upon the ground.

I recollect questioning my friend Kelly about this celebrated charge, at our mess at Windsor in 1816, when he said that he owed his life to the excellence of his charger, which was well bred, very well broke, and of immense power. He thought that with an ordinary horse he would have been killed a hundred times in the numerous encounters which he had to sustain.

The gallant and excellent cavalry officer, Sir Frederick Ponsonby, who greatly distinguished himself at Talavera and many other actions in Spain, was the son of Lord Besborough, and a distant cousin of Sir William Ponsonby who was killed as previously related. He commanded the 12th Light Dragoons, which formed part of Vandeleur's brigade, and made a brilliant charge right through a French brigade of Marcognet's division, and rolled up part of Jacqueminot's lancers, who were in pursuit of the remnant of the Union Brigade. In this most gallant affair, he was struck from his horse by several sabre cuts, run through the body by a lancer as he lay upon the ground, and trampled on by large bodies of cavalry. Ponsonby always considered that he owed his life to a French field-officer, who had brought up some troops to the spot where he lay, had given him a draught of brandy from his flask, and directed one of his men to wrap him in a cloak and place a knapsack under his head.

It is pleasant to think that Ponsonby became acquainted, many years afterward, with his preserver. The Baron de Laussat, formerly deputy for his department, the Basses Pyrenees, and a gentleman universally respected and beloved by all who knew him, was at this time a major in the dragoons of the Imperial Guard. After he had quitted the army, he travelled in the East for some years, and on his return, when at Malta, was introduced to Sir F. Ponsonby, then a major-general and governor of the island. In the course of conversation, the battle of Waterloo was discussed, and on Ponsonby recounting his many narrow escapes, and the kind treatment he had received from the French officer, M. de Laussat said: "Was he not in such-and-such a uniform?"

"He was," said Sir F.

"And did he not say so-and-so to you, and was not the cloak of such-and-such a colour?"

"I remember it perfectly," was the answer.

Several other details were entered into, which I now forget, but which left no doubt upon Ponsonby's mind that he saw before him the man to whom he owed his life.

"I was with the famous Colonel Sourd," added Laussat, "and I only knew that I had rendered what assistance I could to an English officer of rank, who seemed in a very hopeless state; and I am delighted to think that my care was not bestowed in vain."

★★

About two o'clock in the afternoon, Napoleon directed a vigorous attack to be made with the infantry and artillery of D'Erlon's corps against the left wing of the Allies, where Picton, with his 5th division, was gallantly maintaining his ground, Picton at length, seeing the French begin to waver, ordered his men to charge, which they did with effect; but as they drove the enemy back their gallant general received a mortal wound, but died not unavenged.

Several attacks were also made in the course of the day by another portion of D'Erlon's corps against the farm of La Haye Sainte, on the Charleroi road, where some of the German Legion were posted. Three times did the garrison gallantly repel all attempts of the enemy to take it, but upon a fourth attack being made about three o'clock in the afternoon, when the ammunition of the garrison was exhausted, the farm fell temporarily into the possession of the French, whereupon the emperor immediately ordered an attack to be made from this advanced post of his line on the centre of the allied position, and entrusted the duty to Donzelot's and Allix's troops.

For this purpose some French skirmishers from these corps were assembled under the shelter of some low ground west of the farmhouse, who upon advancing from their comparative place of security were enabled to pour a flanking fire into the left flank of the 3rd Battalion First Guards, and the 2nd Battalion 95th Rifles—a fire which became at last so serious that Maitland found it necessary to advance and dislodge them, and being himself in the square, he gave directions to Lieutenant-Colonel D'Oyly, then in command of the battalion, to advance his men. The battalion was, as we have seen, in square, prepared to repel the repeated and constantly recurring attacks of the enemy's cavalry, who were still in the neighbourhood at the foot of the slope, and it would have been hazardous under such circumstances to form line in the usual manner.

The general, therefore, relying upon the steadiness of the men, merely directed the flank faces of the square to be thrown back in sections, and in that formation the 3rd Battalion advanced, being prepared to reform square at the shortest notice. Though this forward and independent movement was necessary, it was not intended to be of long duration; but short as it was, it at once attracted the notice of the batteries on the opposite hills, which, while the battalion was halted and firing into the skirmishers, mowed a passage two or three times through the faces of the square, the French cavalry on the right, all the time threatening another assault.

Nothing daunted by this combined attack of the three arms of the enemy, the men, while continuing their fire with un-shaken steadiness, closed up the gaps thus made in their ranks with promptitude and decision. Maitland having at last forced the enemy's infantry to retire, and finding the fire of their artillery too deadly to be longer resisted, if he remained thus in front of the general line of battle, ordered the battalion to retire about forty yards up the hill, which it did with the greatest coolness; nor did the French Cavalry venture to attack it, either during the advance or during the subsequent return of the battalion over the brow of the hill to its original position, as it would have done had any symptoms of unsteadiness been detected in the ranks of the British Guards.

When the emperor commenced his attacks against Hougoumont, and during their continuance, he ordered a furious cannonade, which was well replied to, to be directed against the other parts of the Anglo allied line, in hopes of shaking it, before he hurled his numerous cavalry against its bristling ranks. The cannonade was very heavy, and the division of Guards, though exposed to its full force, stood it with the utmost steadiness. Their original formation at the commencement of the action was in contiguous column of battalions at quarter distance right to front, but on seeing that the French cavalry were making preparations to attack, they formed squares on their respective leading companies, the Second Battalion First Guards being somewhat in rear of the line of the Third Battalion, and the latter considerably in advance of the general line.

Nothing could exceed the gallantry with which the Imperial

Cavalry of France advanced in immense masses and repeatedly charged the allied squares. After an unsuccessful attempt against the squares of the Guards, they would retire 100 or 150 yards, and again return to the charge, only to be again driven off and decimated by the British bayonet and musketry fire. As wave succeeds wave against an iron-bound coast, only to be broken and thrown back in spray, so did French squadron succeed squadron, only to be hurled back by the fire and bayonet of the British square. Sometimes they would halt at a certain distance and send forward a few skirmishers to fire off their pistols, but the British Guards were too steady to reply to these, and reserved their ammunition for the charge which was sure to follow.

★★

The whole of the British infantry not actually engaged were at that time formed into squares; and as you looked along our lines, it seemed as if we formed a continuous wall of human beings. I should not forget to state that when the enemy's artillery began to play on us, we had orders to lie down; we could hear the shot and shell whistling around us, killing and wounding great numbers; then again, we were ordered on our knees to receive cavalry. The French artillery, which consisted of three hundred guns—we did not muster more than half that number—committed terrible havoc during the early part of the battle, whilst we were acting on the defensive.

The Guards had what in modern battles is called a hot corner of it, and the greatest "gluttons" (and we had many such) must have allowed, when night came on, that they had had fighting enough. I confess that I am to this day astonished that any of us remained alive. From eleven o'clock till seven we were pounded with shot and shell at long and short range, were incessantly potted at by *tirailleurs*, who kept up a most biting fire, constantly charged by immense masses of cavalry, who seemed determined to go in and win, preceded as their visits were by a terrific fire of artillery'.

During the battle our squares presented a shocking sight.

Inside we were nearly suffocated by the smoke and smell from burnt cartridges. It was impossible to move a yard without treading upon a wounded comrade, or upon the bodies of the dead, and the loud groans of the wounded and dying were most appalling.

During the terrible fire of artillery which preceded the repeated charges of the *cuirassiers* against our squares, many shells fell amongst us. We were lying down, when a shell fell between Captain (afterward Colonel) Colquitt and another officer. In an instant Colquitt jumped up, caught up the shell as if it had been a cricket ball, and flung it over the heads of both officers and men, thus saving the lives of many brave fellows.

When I was lying down in square to present a rather less fair mark to the French artillery, which had got very near us, and had caused immense loss in our ranks, a cannon-ball struck the ground close to Algernon Greville and myself, without injuring either of us. At the end of the day, I found that a grape-shot had gone through the top of my shako, and one of my coat-tails had been shot off.

★★

It was now about four o'clock, and the cannonade was very heavy during the interval of the cavalry charges. The two commanding officers of battalions, D'Oyly and Stables were both wounded, and placed *hors de combat*, when the command of the 3rd Battalion devolved upon Lord Saltoun, who had lately joined from Hougomont, and that of the 2nd upon Lieutenant-Colonel Reeve. The two wounded colonels were carried off the field, and Colonel Stables died the following morning.

About the same time Major-General George Cooke, commanding the division of Guards, was obliged to quit the field, so seriously wounded as to necessitate the amputation of his left arm. The command of the division now devolved upon the senior brigadier, Major-General Hon. Sir John Byng, (the future Earl of Strafford and Colonel of the Coldstream Guards), who, very shortly after four o'clock, rode over from the Second to the

First Brigade, just before the next attack of the enemy's cavalry, in time to witness the steady manner in which the 1st Brigade received the several charges to which it was exposed.

Major-General Maitland, who had been most of the day with the 3rd Battalion of the First Guards, which had been the most exposed, says of the 2nd Battalion that it was continually supporting the 3rd, and was repelling the French cavalry throughout the day with the same unshaken perseverance.

The duke now often looked to the left, to ascertain if the Prussians would soon be coming to his assistance, for the repelling of these constant and desperate attacks was causing a fearful loss in the British and allied ranks. It was indeed to this that Napoleon trusted for eventual success, for well aware of the acknowledged bravery of the British, he calculated on thus wearying them into defeat; but when he saw his cavalry were driven back from these impenetrable squares; and British battalions, though decimated by his artillery, yet showing a perfect front, and still holding their original ground, he could not help exclaiming, "How beautifully those English fight! but they must give way." He was, however, to be bitterly undeceived—firmly, as though rooted to the ground, did they to the last continue to maintain the posts entrusted to them.

★★★

Ney now received orders to attack La Haye Sainte, which was taken about four o'clock. At the same hour Bülow's first columns made their appearance, and attacked D'Erlon and Lobau. I recollect distinctly being able to see Bonaparte and his staff; and some of my brother officers using the glass, exclaimed, "There he is on his white horse."

The enemy's artillery in front of us ceased firing all of a sudden, and we saw large masses of cavalry advance: not a man present who survived could have forgotten in after life the awful *grandeur* of that charge. You perceived at a distance what appeared to be an overwhelming long moving line, which, ever advancing, glittered like a stormy wave of the sea when it catches the sunlight. On came the mounted host until they got near enough, whilst the very earth seemed to vibrate beneath their thundering tramp. One might suppose that nothing could have resisted the shock of this terrible moving mass. They were the famous *cuirassiers*, almost all old soldiers. In an almost incredibly short period, they were within twenty yards of us, shouting *"Vive l'empereur!"* The word of command, "Prepare to receive cavalry," had been given, every man in the front ranks knelt, and a wall bristling with steel, held together by steady hands, presented itself to the infuriated *cuirassiers*.

The artillery did great execution, but our musketry did not at first seem to kill many men, though it brought down a large number of horses, and created indescribable confusion. The horses of the first rank of *cuirassiers*, in spite of all the efforts of their riders, came to a standstill, shaking and covered with foam, at about twenty yards' distance from our squares, and generally resisted all attempts to force them to charge the line of serried steel. On one occasion two gallant French officers forced their way into a gap momentarily created by the discharge of artillery: one was killed by Staples, the other by Adair. Nothing could be more gallant than the behaviour of those veterans, many of whom had distinguished themselves on half the battlefields of Europe.

Our square was a perfect hospital, being full of dead, dying, and mutilated soldiers. The charges of cavalry were in appearance very formidable, but in reality, a great relief, as the artillery could no longer fire on us. The very earth shook under the enormous mass of men and horses. I never shall forget the strange noise our bullets made against the breastplates of Kellermann's and Milhaud's *cuirassiers*, six or seven thousand in number, who attacked us with great fury. I can only compare it, with a somewhat homely simile, to the noise of a violent hailstorm beating upon panes of glass.

In the midst of our terrible fire their officers were seen as if on parade, keeping order in their ranks, and encouraging them. Unable to renew the charge, but unwilling to retreat, they brandished their swords with loud cries of *"Vive l'Empereur!"* and allowed themselves to be mowed down by hundreds rather than yield. Our men, who shot them down, could not help admiring the gallant bearing and heroic resignation of their enemies.

I should observe that just before this charge the duke entered by one of the angles of the square, accompanied only by one *aide-de-camp*, all the rest of his staff being either killed or wounded. Our commander-in-chief, as far as I could judge, appeared perfectly composed, but looked very thoughtful and pale. He was dressed in a grey great-coat with a cape, white cravat, leather pantaloons, Hessian boots, and a large cocked hat *à la Russe*.

The charge of the French cavalry was gallantly executed; but our well-directed fire brought men and horses down, and ere long the utmost confusion arose in their ranks. The officers were exceedingly brave, and by their gestures and fearless bearing did all in their power to encourage their men to form again and renew the attack. The duke sat unmoved, mounted on his favourite charger. I recollect his asking Colonel Stanhope what o'clock it was, upon which Stanhope took out his watch, and said it was twenty minutes past four. The duke replied, "The battle is mine; and if the Prussians arrive soon, there will be an end to the war.

About the same time, Saltoun and Charley Ellis, who had commanded the light companies of the battalions of Guards, joined us with the wreck of those detachments, after their gallant defence of Hougoumont. I well remember General Maitland saying to Saltoun, "Your defence saved the army; nothing could be more gallant. Every man of you deserves promotion." Saltoun replied that it was "touch and go—a matter of life and death—for all within the walls had sworn that they would never surrender;" and Gunthorpe the adjutant added, "Our officers were determined never to yield, and the men were resolved to stand by them to the last."

Soon after the *cuirassiers* had retired, we observed to our right the red hussars of the *Garde Impériale* charging a square of Brunswick riflemen, who were about fifty yards from us. This charge was brilliantly executed, but the well-sustained fire from the square baffled the enemy, who were obliged to retire after suffering a severe loss in killed and wounded. The ground was completely covered with those brave men, who lay in various positions, mutilated in every conceivable way. Among the fallen we perceived the gallant colonel of the hussars lying under his horse, which had been killed.

All of a sudden two riflemen of the Brunswickers left their battalion, and after taking from their helpless victim his purse, watch, and other articles of value, they deliberately put the colonel's pistols to the poor fellow's head, and blew out his brains. "Shame! shame!" was heard from our ranks, and a feeling of indignation ran through the whole line; but the deed was done: this brave soldier lay a lifeless corpse in sight of his cruel foes, whose only excuse perhaps was that their sovereign, the Duke of Brunswick, had been killed two days before by the French at Quatre Bras.

Again, and again various cavalry regiments, heavy dragoons, lancers, hussars, *carabineers* of the Guard, endeavoured to break our walls of steel. The enemy's cavalry had to advance over ground which was so heavy that they could not reach us except at a trot; they therefore came upon us in a much more compact mass than they probably would have done if the ground had been more favourable. When they got within ten or fifteen yards they discharged their carbines, to the cry of "*Vive l'empereur!*" but their fire produced little effect, as is generally the case with the fire of cavalry. Our men had orders not to fire unless they could do so on a near mass; the object being to economise our ammunition, and not to waste it on scattered soldiers. The result was, that when the cavalry had discharged their carbines, and were still far off, we occasionally stood face to face, looking at each other inactively, not knowing what the next move might be.

The lancers were particularly troublesome, and approached

us with the utmost daring. On one occasion I remember, the enemy's artillery having made a gap in the square, the lancers were evidently waiting to avail themselves of it, to rush among us, when Colonel Staples, at once observing their intention, with the utmost promptness filled up the gap, and thus again completed our impregnable steel wall; but in this act he fell mortally wounded. The cavalry seeing this, made no attempt to carry out their original intentions, and observing that we had entirely regained our square, confined themselves to hovering round us.

I must not forget to mention that the lancers in particular never failed to despatch our wounded, whenever they had an opportunity of doing so. When we received cavalry, the order was to fire low; so that on the first discharge of musketry, the ground was strewed with the fallen horses and their riders, which impeded the advance of those behind them, and broke the shock of the charge. It was pitiable to witness the agony of the poor horses, which really seemed conscious of the dangers that surrounded them: we often saw a poor wounded animal raise its head, as if looking for its rider to afford him aid. There is nothing perhaps amongst the episodes of a great battle more striking than the debris of a cavalry charge, where men and horses are seen scattered and wounded on the ground in every variety of painful attitude. Many a time the heart sickened at the moaning tones of agony which came from man, and scarcely less intelligent horse, as they lay in fearful agony upon the field of battle.

★★

The Prussians at length began to make their appearance on the field near Planchenoit, to the right and right rear of the French, and Napoleon was now pressed by them on that flank. In vain had he endeavoured with his cavalry to shake the British squares; in vain had he stormed again and again the stronghold of Hougomont on the British right; in vain had he attempted to force Picton on their left. Most of his troops had been baffled, but there still remained to him one more chance of retrieving the fortunes of the day; he still fondly hoped that the hour of his triumph was at hand, and that he should be able once more to grasp as firmly as ever the sceptre of Imperial France. He resolved to organise the columns of Grenadiers and *Chasseurs* of his Imperial Guards, and hurl them against the centre of the allied position, where stood firmly as a rock Maitland's 1st Brigade of British Guards.

The following anecdote referring to this period is recorded of Lord Saltoun by an intimate friend, and his former adjutant. During a lull, just after the repulse of one attack and before the final one, the duke was on his horse close to the 1st Brigade, and after looking carefully with his glass along the whole of the French position, turned to those of his staff near him, saying, "Well, I think they are pretty well told out now."

Saltoun immediately said to one of the staff officers, "I don't know; when I was outside the wood at Hougoumont, this morning, before the action began, I watched a column of men, as far as I can guess about 5,000 or 6,000, go into a hollow opposite; I have kept my eye on this spot all day, and have never seen them come out yet."

Upon this being repeated to the duke, he turned his glass in that direction, and after a moment's pause said, "By God, he is right! they are coming out now;" and it is said that the duke was so much struck with the coolness and power of observation exhibited by Lord Saltoun under such circumstances, that he ever afterwards spoke of him as a thorough soldier.

When the duke saw the storm impending over the centre of the position, he directed that the space to the right of the First Guards, left vacant by detaching the 2nd Brigade to Hougoumont, should be occupied by Adams' brigade consisting of the 52nd, 71st, and 95th Regiments. Part of that brigade had been posted there at the time of the advance of the 3rd Battalion First Guards against the skirmishers near La Haye Sainte, but had resumed its previous position at the same time as the 3rd Battalion did so. The 52nd, with the 71st and 95th Regiments, now resumed that more advanced position, but they had not an opportunity of taking part in the defeat of the first column of attack.

For an hour before carrying out his plan, Napoleon directed a furious concentrated fire from the whole of his artillery, upon that portion of the allied position lying between the farm of Hougoumont and La Haye Sainte. Fortunately, there ran along this part of the field of battle a cart road, on one side of which was a ditch and bank. In and under cover of these, the 1st Brigade of Guards sheltered themselves during this terrific cannonade, which lasted about three-quarters of an hour, and without its protection the two battalions must have been annihilated. Napoleon probably calculated on such an effect, but he had yet to learn the extent of British fortitude and endurance.

The duke was well aware of the enemy's intentions, and being at this time close to the two battalions of the First Guards, which at first were in squares, and with which he remained during the subsequent attack, he desired General Maitland to form them into line four deep, as he thought it possible that Napoleon would support the attack with his cavalry. Maitland immediately carried out the duke's order, covering his change of formation with a line of skirmishers under Swinburn, who only rejoined his battalion a few moments before the enemy was upon them. The formation into line, instead of being made by deployment, was effected by simply wheeling up to the front, the four-deep flank faces of the square, the rear faces forming the extremities of each battalion, so that the grenadier companies were in the centre, and the men could more readily form square again, should circumstances require it. The whole brigade as it now stood, four deep, occupied only the length of one battalion in line.

Major-General Byng was also present with the First Brigade at this period of the action, but as a true gentleman, not wishing to take away from Maitland the credit of commanding such troops on such an occasion, he wrote in his despatch the following day, that neither his presence nor his advice was required, and that he only stayed with him as a humble individual, adding, that Maitland's own gallantry and judgment directed all that was necessary.

The above formation was scarcely completed, and the men ordered to lie down again, when, at a quarter past seven, the furious cannonade suddenly ceased. As the smoke gradually cleared away, under cover of which Napoleon had been organising his attack, near La Belle Alliance, a superb sight opened upon the brigade. Close columns of regiments of the Old Imperial Guard, 5,000 strong, directed by Napoleon himself, and led by Ney, on foot, (for his horse had been shot under him,) were seen advancing up the slope *au pas de charge* direct upon them, with shouts of "*Vive l'Empereur!*"

These columns were composed of the infantry regiments of the Old Imperial Guard, under the command respectively of Generals Christiani, Poret, and Harlet, all in line of battalion close columns, forming a front of three companies. The 1st Regiment of Grenadiers of the Guard, 1,300 strong, remained in reserve on the heights of La Belle Alliance, and General Count Friant, the Colonel and Commander-in-Chief of the Old Guard, remained with this regiment on the heights.

As the leading columns, apparently as regularly formed as for a field day, began to ascend the incline on the top of which the British First Guards were posted, they became exposed to the concentrated artillery fire of the right wing of the Allies, by which they suffered much. Notwithstanding this, they continued their advance in admirable order, and with the greatest enthusiasm, preceded by a cloud of skirmishers; but these were soon driven back upon their main body by a fire of canister, grape, and shrapnel shells, delivered at a distance of less than 100 yards. At first, their astonishment, these columns met no enemy to offer any obstruction to their further progress, when, after arrive within from twenty to thirty yards of the position occupied by the First Guards, they suddenly saw rise up before them what proved to be to them an impenetrable barrier.

The duke now gave directions to Maitland, saying:

"Now, Maitland, now's your time," and immediately the men

were ordered to rise. They had already been warned to reserve their fire till the enemy should arrive within a very short distance. It was, as Siborne relates, a moment of thrilling excitement. The First Guards, springing up suddenly, in a most compact four-deep line, appeared to the enemy as starting out of the ground. The Imperial Guard, with their high bonnets, as they crowned the summit of ridge, appeared to the British, through the smoky haze of the battlefield, like a corps of giants advancing upon them. The British Guards instantly opened their fire with a tremendous volley, thrown in with great coolness and precision, and the enemy were then so close upon them, some only fifteen yards, that the men would fire without putting their muskets to the shoulder, while to accelerate the subsequent file firing the rear ranks passed their loaded muskets to the front.

An oblique fire was poured in upon the right flank of the advancing column by the 33rd and 69th British Regiments, which had been promptly pushed forward by Halket on the left of the Guards. The head of the column, surprised at this sudden apparition, halted, and the entire mass staggered under the effect of the murderous fire poured into them at such close quarters. In less than a minute, more than three hundred of the "*Veille Garde*" fell to rise no more, but the high spirit and innate valour of the Imperial Guard were not to be subdued by a first repulse; their officers, placing themselves in the front and on the flanks, called aloud, waved with their swords, and by words and gestures attempted a deployment into line, in order to acquire a more extended front; but the head of the column being continually shattered and driven back by the well-sustained fire of the Guards within so limited a space, the attempt was fruitless.

The confusion into which the enemy's columns were now thrown became every moment more manifest, and the duke, seizing the opportunity, ordered Maitland to charge, which order was instantly obeyed. At the same tune Saltoun, equally alive to the real state of the enemy's columns, shouted to his battalion, "Now's the time, my boys." The brigade answered with a cheer, and led by Maitland, Saltoun, Reeve, and Gunthorpe, who placed themselves in front, sprang forward to the charge, and as they continued down the hill in pursuit of the Imperial Guard, they passed over a hedge of dead and dying bodies that lay in front of the position they had so gloriously defended.

Many Frenchmen nearest their pursuers threw down their arms and knapsacks, and dispersed, and a panic seizing the men as they returned towards La Belle Alliance, whence a short half hour before they had started in all the pomp and majesty of war, the mass appeared to dissolve into a confused horde of human beings.

General Maitland, referring to this first charge of the Imperial Guard, says:

> The moment they (the French) appeared and began to form (deploy) about twenty yards in our front, we poured in the most deadly fire that perhaps was ever witnessed, as the field of battle abundantly testified the following morning. The Imperial Guard retreated, the whole of our line advanced, and the rest on the part of the enemy was all flight.

★★

But here we came to the end of our long and fiery ordeal and, last of all, we were attacked by *"la Vieille Garde"* itself. The French veterans, conspicuous by their high bearskin caps and lofty stature, on breasting the ridge behind which we were at that time, were met by a fearful fire of artillery and musketry, which swept away whole masses of those valiant soldiers.

It was about five o'clock on that memorable day, that we suddenly received orders to retire behind an elevation in our rear. The enemy's artillery had come up *en masse* within a hundred yards of us. By the time they began to discharge their guns, however, we were lying down behind the rising ground, and protected by the ridge before referred to. The enemy's cavalry was in the rear of their artillery, in order to be ready to protect it if attacked; but no attempt was made on our part to do so. After they had pounded away at us for about half an hour, they deployed, and up came the whole mass of the Imperial infantry of the Guard, led on by the emperor in person.

We had now before us probably about twenty thousand of the best soldiers in France, the heroes of many memorable victories; we saw the bearskin caps rising higher and higher, as they ascended the ridge of ground which separated us, and advanced nearer and nearer to our lines.

It was at this moment that the Duke of Wellington gave his famous order for our bayonet charge, as he rode along the line; these are the precise words he made use of: "Guards, get up and charge!" We were instantly on our legs, and after so many hours of inaction and irritation at maintaining a purely defensive attitude—all the time suffering the loss of comrades and friends—the spirit which animated officers and men may easily be imagined. After firing a volley as soon as the enemy were within shot, we rushed on with fixed bayonets, and that hearty hurrah peculiar to British soldiers.

It appeared that our men, deliberately and with calculation, singled out their victims; for as they came upon the Imperial Guard our line broke, and the fighting became irregular. The impetuosity of our men seemed almost to paralyse their enemies: I witnessed several of the Imperial Guard who were run through the body apparently without any resistance on their parts. I observed a big Welshman of the name of Hughes, who was six feet seven inches in height, run through with his bayonet, and knock down with the butt-end of his firelock, I should think a dozen at least of his opponents. This terrible contest did not last more than ten minutes, for the Imperial Guard was soon in full retreat, leaving all their guns and many prisoners in our hands. In disorder, they were charged by us with complete success, and driven in utter rout and discomfiture down the ravine. The Prussians having now arrived in force on the French right, a general advance of the whole line was ordered, and the day was won.

The famous General Cambronne was taken prisoner fighting hand to hand with the gallant Sir Colin Halkett, who was shortly after shot through the cheeks. Cambronne's supposed answer of *"La Garde ne se rend pas"* was an invention of after times, and he himself always denied having used such an expression. Sir C. Halkett's wound, which was from a musket ball through the jaws, was not so dangerous; for it was said by Forbes, the surgeon, that the general must have been in the act of ordering his men to charge, with his mouth open when he was struck.

★★★

As the brigade continued its pursuit down the slope, in the direction of La Belle Alliance, its right flank became exposed to n second column, the *Chasseurs* of the Imperial Guard, who were advancing, but too late, from a point nearer to the enclosure of Hougoumont, to the support of their brethren of the first column. Maitland, perceiving this, and seeing that his right flank might be turned, halted, and ordered the right wing of the second battalion to be thrown back, so as to be parallel with the line of advance of the French column. In the midst of this manoeuvre the third battalion, mistaking the word of command, *halt, front, form up* for *form square*, commenced that formation, expecting the enemy's cavalry to be down on them. The mistake, however, was soon rectified, and in a few moments the brigade was again near its former position, in a four-deep line, with its left thrown a little forward, ready to repel this second attacking column of the Imperial Guards.

Meanwhile Adams, having brought his brigade to the ground formerly occupied by the second Brigade of Guards, had formed his line, throwing forward his right shoulder, the second battalion 95th on the left, then the 52nd and the 71st on the right, extending towards Hougoumont. As the second column of the *Chasseurs* of the Imperial Guard advanced up the slope in similar formation to the First, it was received by Adams' Brigade, which poured a destructive fire into its left flank, and was met in front by the direct fire of the First Guards, who had thrown forward their left; to be more directly opposed to the advancing columns.

This flank fire of Adams' Brigade mainly contributed to the final overthrow of the second column, and as the Duke of Wellington saw it begin to waver, he ordered a general advance of the whole line; Adams' Brigade followed this second column, while the First Guards, under Maitland followed the track of the first column, till it reached the Charleroi road, near La Belle Alliance. Here the First Regiment of Grenadiers of the old French Imperial Guards, that had been left in reserve, attempted, after forming square to stem the flying torrent and its pursuers; but to no avail; it shared the fate of the other regiments, broke, and nought remained of the Army of Imperial France but a confused mass of soldiery, which during the whole following night, continued a disorderly retreat, pursued by the avenging Prussians.

As to the supposed historical reply of the French Guard, *"La Garde meurt, mais ne se rend pas!"* General Cambronne, who commanded part of it, did surrender, and was made prisoner by the British Guards; and it was Lord Saltoun himself who, at the moment of his surrender, gave him in charge to a tall grenadier named Kent, who conducted him to Brussels.

The First Guards, having pursued as far as the Charleroi road, formed into column, and continued their advance along the *chaussée*, through the whole depth of the late French position, and bivouacked for the night in the fields on the right, two miles in advance of the position of Waterloo.

★★★

The Honourable George Damer was on the staff at Waterloo, and, toward the close of the day, was sent to order the Union Brigade to advance with the rest of the army. After a long search, he at last came upon all that remained of the brave fellows that composed the brigade. They were reduced to about two hundred and fifty men; many of them wounded, with heads and hands bandaged, were standing by their horses, who were panting and blowing, and looked completely done up.

At their head stood the gallant Colonel Muter of the Inniskillings, upon whom the command of the brigade had fallen after Ponsonby's death. This grim veteran had his helmet beaten in, and his arm, which had been badly wounded, was in a sling. When Damer came up, and said, "Now, gentlemen, you are to advance with the rest of the army," he said he should never forget the look that Muter cast upon him. The gallant Scot, however, said nothing, but got his men together, and they all broke into a sort of canter, and, guided by Damer, came upon some French infantry, who were still defending themselves with a kind of desperation. As Muter gave the order to charge, the French fired a volley and hit Damer in the knee, who heard Muter grumble out in his Scotch phraseology, as he dashed amongst the French, "I think you ha' it nu', sir."

After our own regiment's final charge, and the retreat of the French Army, we arrived and bivouacked about nine o'clock in the orchard of the farm of La Belle Alliance about a hundred yards from the farmhouse where Napoleon had remained for some hours. We were presently disturbed by the sound of trumpets; I immediately hurried off, in company with several other officers, and found that the sound proceeded from a Prussian cavalry regiment with Blücher at its head. The Duke of Wellington, who had given rendezvous to Blücher at this spot, then rode up, and the two victorious generals shook hands in the most cordial and hearty manner. After a short conversation, our chief rode off to Brussels, while Blücher and the Prussians joined their own army, which, under General Gneisenau, was already in hot pursuit of the French. After this I entered the farmhouse where Napoleon had passed part of the day. The furniture had to all appearance been destroyed, but I found an immense fire made of a wooden bedstead and the legs of chairs, which appeared by the embers to have been burning for a considerable length of time.

★★★

Nearly the whole of the enemy's artillery, 122 guns, fell into the hands of the victors.

Such a triumph was not gained without great losses. The British and Hanoverians alone lost in killed 116 officers and 1,931 men, the proportion of British being 1,754. In wounded they lost 504 officers and 6,512 men, of the British lost 5,892,

The losses of the two battalions of First Guards, both at Quatre Bras and at Waterloo, show a total loss in the regiment during those two days, in killed and wounded, of 1,034 men.

★★★

The losses and severely wounded among my fellow officers of the First Guards were many and tragic. No language can express the admiration felt by all who witnessed the heroic exploits of poor Captain Adair of our regiment. During the charges of the French cavalry, which were always preceded by a tremendous fire of artillery at point blank distance, we lost many men. The *cuirassiers* and heavy dragoons approached so close that it was feared they would enter by the gap which had been made in our square. Adair rushed forward, placed himself in the open space, and, with one blow of his sword, killed a French officer who had actually got amongst our men. After many exploits, showing a coolness and a courage rarely equalled, and never surpassed, Adair was struck toward the end of the day by a cannon-ball, which shattered his thigh near the hip. His sufferings during the amputation were dreadful; the shot had torn away the flesh of the thigh, and the bones were sticking up near the hip in splinters.

The surgeon, Mr. Gilder, had much difficulty in using his knife, having blunted it and all his other instruments by amputations in the earlier part of the battle. Poor Adair during the operation had sufficient pluck to make one last ghastly joke, saying, "Take your time, Mr. Carver." He soon afterward died from loss of blood.

Ensign Somerville Burges, of the 1st Foot Guards was a younger son of Sir James Bland Burges. (His elder brother was killed at Burgos in Spain.) He enjoyed soldiering in the real sense of the word, and sought glory on every field of battle.

He entered the Guards before he attained the age of seventeen, and his buoyant spirits and athletic frame fitted him for a military life. I breakfasted with him on the morning of the battle. After many acts of great personal courage, he was wounded by a cannon-ball, which shattered his leg in a frightful manner. Amputation was the consequence; and after the surgeon had dressed the wounds, he hailed some soldiers to carry Burges to the cart, upon which the latter declined being carried, saying, "I will hop into it; "and he succeeded in performing this extraordinary feat without further injury to the wounded stump. This heroic soldier, owing to the regulations then in force, was put on the shelf for the remainder of his life.

The wound which Captain Percival received was one of the most painful it ever fell to a soldier's lot to bear. He received a ball which carried away all his teeth and both his jaws, and left nothing on the mouth but the skin of the cheeks. Percival recovered sufficiently to join our regiment in the Tower, three years subsequent to the Battle of Waterloo. He had to be fed with porridge and a few spoonsful of broth; but notwithstanding all the care to preserve his life, he sunk from inanition, and died very shortly after, his body presenting the appearance of a skeleton.

Among the many episodes of a battlefield, there is none so touching as the last moments of a brave soldier. Captain Curzon, son of Lord Scarsdale, was on the staff, and received a mortal wound toward the end of the battle, and lay bleeding to death by the side of his favourite charger, one of whose legs had been shattered by a cannon-ball. As Lord March was passing by, Curzon had just strength to call to him, "Get me help, my dear March, for I fear it is all over with me."

Lord March hastened to look for a surgeon, and found one belonging to the first battalion of our regiment, who went to the poor fellow's assistance; but, alas! life was extinct before the doctor arrived. The doctor, in relating this event to us afterward, said:

"I found poor Curzon dead, leaning his head upon the neck

of his favourite horse, which seemed to be aware of the death of his master, so quiet did it remain, as if afraid to disturb his last sleep. As I approached, it neighed feebly, and looked at me as if it wanted relief from the pain of its shattered limb, so I told a soldier to shoot it through the head to put it out of its pain. The horse as well as its master were both old acquaintances of mine, and I was quite upset by the sight of them lying dead together."

This tribute of sympathy and feeling was the more remarkable as coming from the doctor who was one of the hardest and roughest diamonds I ever remember to have known; but on this occasion something moved him, and he had tears in his eyes as he related the incident

★★★

No time was lost, the day after the battle, in following up the scattered hosts of France, and moving on its capital, for the Duke of Wellington gave orders to continue the forward movement without delay; according to which the Guards were *en route* at an early hour, and in the course of the day reached Nivelles, the same town they had traversed in another direction only three days before, on their road to Quatre Bras. The duke himself arrived there the same evening.

★★★

Early on the morning after the Battle of Waterloo, I visited Hougoumont, in order to witness with my own eyes, the traces of one of the most hotly contested spots of the field of battle. I came first upon the orchard, and there discovered heaps of dead men, in various uniforms: those of the Guards in their usual red jackets, the German Legion in green, and the French dressed in blue, mingled together. The dead and the wounded positively covered the whole area of the orchard; not less than two thousand men had there fallen. The apple-trees presented a singular appearance; shattered branches were seen hanging about their mother-trunks in such profusion, that one might almost suppose the stiff-growing and stunted tree had been converted into the willow: every tree was riddled and smashed in a manner which told that the showers of shot had been incessant. On this spot I lost some of my dearest and bravest friends, and the country had to mourn many of its most heroic sons slain here.

I must observe that, according to the custom of commanding officers, whose business it is after a great battle to report to the commander-in-chief, the muster-roll of fame always closes before the rank of captain. It has always appeared to me a great injustice that there should ever be any limit to the roll of gallantry of either officers or men. If a captain, lieutenant, an ensign, a sergeant, or a private, has distinguished himself for his bravery, his intelligence, or both, their deeds ought to be reported, in order that the sovereign and nation should know who really fight the great battles of England. Of the class of officers and men to which I have referred, there were many even of superior rank who were omitted to be mentioned in the public despatches.

Thus, for example, to the individual courage of Lord Saltoun and Charley Ellis, who commanded the light companies, was mainly owing our success at Hougoumont. The same may be said of Needham, Percival, Erskine, Grant, Vyner, Buckley, Master, and young Algernon Greville, who at that time could not have been more than seventeen years old. Excepting Percival, whose jaws were torn away by a grape-shot, every one of these heroes miraculously escaped.

I do not wish, in making these observations, to detract from the bravery and skill of officers whose names have already been mentioned in official despatches, but I think it only just that the services of those I have particularised should not be forgotten by one of their companions in arms.

We had not advanced for many minutes before we met several of our gallant companions in arms who had been wounded. They were lying in wagons of the country, and had been abandoned by the drivers. Some of these poor fellows belonged to our regiment, and, on passing close to one of the wagons, a man cried out, "For God's sake, Mr. Gronow, give us some water or we shall go mad." I did not hesitate for a moment, but jumped into the cart, and gave the poor fellow all the water my flask contained. The other wounded soldiers then entreated me to fill it with some muddy water which they had descried in a neighbouring ditch, half filled by the rain of the preceding day. As I thought a flask would be of little use among so many, I took off my shako, and having first stopped up with my belcher handkerchief a hole which a musket-ball had made in the top of it, filled it with water several times for these poor fellows, who were all too severely wounded to have got it for themselves, and who drank it off with tears of delight.

About twelve o'clock, on the second day after the Battle of Waterloo, when on our march to Paris, we were ordered to come to a halt. Every officer and soldier immediately set to work to get rid of the superabundance of beard which had been suffered to grow for several days. During this not very agreeable duty, a shout was heard from Lord Saltoun, who called us to witness a bet he had made with Bob Ellison, that he, Ellison, could not shave off his beard in one minute.

Preparations were made, Ellison taking care to bathe his face for a considerable time in water. He then commenced operations, and, in less than a minute, and without the aid of a looking-glass, actually won his bet (a considerable one), to the astonishment, and, I must add, the satisfaction of his comrades. This feat appeared to us all perfectly impossible to accomplish, as his face was covered with the stubble of a week's growth of hair, so dark that it had procured for him in the regiment the sobriquet of Black Bob.

Ellison was one of our best officers. After joining the brigade at Cadiz, he was present in every action in the Peninsula, and was with the light companies at Hougoumont. He greatly distinguished himself there; and on one occasion, when he was forced to retreat from the orchard to the *château*, he would have been bayoneted by the French, had not the men, with whom he was a great favourite, charged back, and saved his life. Ellison led the storming party at Péronne, and commanded the second battalion of his regiment in Canada. He was colonel of his old battalion in 1843; when, at a brigade field-day in Hyde Park, on the occasion of a general salute, as he gave the word "Present arms," he dropped down dead from his horse, while the old corps, in which he had passed nearly forty years, were presenting arms to him.

All who knew him will bear witness with me to his many amiable and excellent qualities. In his younger days he was remarkably good-looking, and he had still preserved his handsome face and kindly, expressive eye. Though quick and clever, no one ever heard him say a malevolent or ill-natured thing. If there was a good turn to be done, or a friendly word to be spoken, Black Bob was first and foremost; and in looking back on the old friends and comrades of bygone days, I feel there is not one I could name who was more deservedly popular or more generally regretted than Colonel Ellison.

★★

The army continued its advance on the 20th, and while part was directed on Mons, the Guards, following the high road from Nivelles, proceeded to Binche; and on the 21st reached Bavay, the duke's headquarters being at Malplaquet. Here he was near the frontiers of France, and before crossing them he warned the army that it was entering a country with whose present ruler the allied sovereigns were on friendly terms. On the 22nd the right of the army marched to Le Cateau Cambresis, the Guards to Gourmignies. The weather had continued very wet ever since the action of the 18th and the 23rd was now made a day of rest to most of the army, in order to allow stragglers to rejoin, and ammunition and baggage to be brought up, as well as to enable the duke to take the necessary steps to get possession of Cambrai and Peronne.

The three First Divisions of the army were still near Le Cateau on the 24th, the First Guards being at Bussigny, where the French King, Louis XVIII., came up to them. On the 25th, the First and Third Divisions, with the Dutch-Belgic Infantry, advanced and were encamped at Premont, near Serain; while the Fourth Division occupied Cambrai, which surrendered to them that evening. On the morning of the 26th of June, as Sir John Byng was passing the village of Vermand, where the main body of the duke's army lay, he learnt that the duke himself was there and waited on him. The duke at once exclaimed:

"You are the very person I wish to see; I want you to take Peronne; you may as well take with you the Brigade of Guards and a Dutch-Belgian brigade. I shall be there almost as soon as yourself."

Peronne was distant about eleven miles from the Guards' then position. Byng having given the necessary instructions to Maitland's Brigade of First Guards, and to a Dutch-Belgian brigade, the former marched off at once, and reached Peronne at the same time as the duke, who immediately summoned the garrison, and proceeded to reconnoitre the fortress in person. Believing that it could be taken by storm, he gave orders to prepare for an assault, and directed the attack to be made upon a hornwork which covers the suburbs on the left bank of the Somme. To the Third Battalion First Guards, preceded by the light companies of the First Brigade under Lord Saltoun, was given the task of assaulting the place, while the Second Battalion carried the fascines.

As the Guards advanced, they separated into two columns of attack, the left one destined to scale the left face of the right demi-bastion; the right one to force an entrance by the ravelin and through the gate, which was blown open by the Engineers.

Saltoun immediately rushed to the assault with his light companies, which experienced some slight loss as they crossed the ditch, while Saltoun himself was struck by a grape shot as he was mounting the scaling ladder, but fortunately the shot, striking a purse full of coins, in his pocket, lessened the blow, so that it inflicted but slight injury, and he refused to report himself

PERONNE

wounded.

The hornwork was carried with little loss, and a Dutch brigade of four 9-pounders being brought up and established to the east of the town, to take in reverse the face to be attacked, a few shots were exchanged; while a brigade of four field-pieces was placed so as to command the front of the hornwork itself. After a short interval General Byng sent forward Lieutenant-Colonel Stanhope, his acting quartermaster-general, with a flag of truce, upon which the garrison capitulated, and the maiden fortress surrendered to the Guards, on condition of the men being allowed to go to their homes.

★★★

The fourth or fifth day after Waterloo, we arrived before Péronne la Pucelle (the Virgin town), as the inhabitants delighted to call it; for they boasted that it had never been taken by an enemy. The Duke of Wellington suddenly made his appearance in our bivouac, and gave orders that we should, at all risks, take Péronne before night. We accordingly prepared for action, and commenced proceedings by battering the gates with a strong fire of artillery. The guns of the Virgin fortress returned the compliment, and the first shot from the town fell under the belly of the duke's horse, but beyond knocking the gravel and stones about in all directions, did no injury.

The garrison consisted of fifteen hundred National Guards, who had sworn never to surrender to mortal man; but when these ardent volunteers saw our redcoats coming in with a rush and with a grim determination to take no denial, they wisely laid down their arms and capitulated. Our loss, on this occasion, amounted to nine killed and thirty wounded. Lord Saltoun had a narrow escape; a ball struck him on his breeches pocket, where half a dozen five-*franc* pieces broke the force of the blow. Saltoun, though not very Buonapartist in his opinions, retained the mark of the emperor's effigy on his thigh for some time, and though not returned as wounded, suffered great pain for several days after.

★★★

As General Byng was returning to Vermand to report to the duke the capture of the fortress, he met about halfway the tardy Dutch-Belgian brigade, which had been ordered at the same time as the Guards to proceed to the front.

The two battalions of the First Guards encamped at Peronne that night, while the Second Brigade with its headquarters halted at Caulaincourt. The First Brigade did not long remain in charge of their last capture, for two battalions of the Dutch-Belgian brigade, which had arrived too late to take part in the storming of that fortress, were ordered on the following day to occupy it, while the First Brigade of Guards, with the remainder of the Dutch brigade, marched through Nesle to the village of Crescy, and rejoined the first corps, bivouacking at Caulaincourt.

The necessary delay experienced by the duke in taking Cambrai and Peronne, and waiting for supplies, caused him to be one day in rear of the Prussians. On the 28th, the First Corps marched upon Couchy, and the next day by Estrées St. Denis along the *chaussée* to St. Martin Longeau, where the Guards encamped, being then thirty-five miles from Paris, while the advanced posts of the British Army were already at Senlis, ten miles further.

★★

We perceived, on entering France, that our Allies the Prussians had committed fearful atrocities on the defenceless inhabitants of the villages and farms which lay in their line of march. Before we left La Belle Alliance, I had already seen the brutality of some of the Prussian infantry, who hacked and cut up, in a most savage manner, all the cows and pigs which were in the farmyards, placing upon their bayonets the still quivering flesh, and roasting it on the coals. On our line of march, whenever we arrived at towns or villages through which the Prussians had passed, we found that every article of furniture in the houses had been destroyed in the most wanton manner; looking-glasses, mahogany bedsteads, pictures, beds, and

155

mattresses had been hacked, cut, half burned, and scattered about in every direction, and, on the slightest remonstrance of the wretched inhabitants, they were beaten in a most shameful manner, and sometimes shot. It is true that the Prussians owed the French a long debt of vengeance for all the atrocities committed by the French at Berlin, particularly by Davoust's corps after the Battle of Jena.

On the Guards arriving at St. Pont Maixans, a town situated at about forty miles from Paris, I was sent by the adjutant to look out for quarters for myself and servant. In the neighbourhood of a small wood, I perceived a mill, and near it a river, and on looking a little further, saw a large farmhouse. This I entered, but could not discover any living being. My servant, who had gone upstairs, however, informed me that the farmer was lying in bed dreadfully wounded from numerous sabre cuts. I approached his bed, and he appeared more dead than alive; but on my questioning him, he said the Prussians had been there the night before, had violated and carried off his three daughters, had taken away his cart-horses and cattle, and because he had no money to give them, they had tied him to his bed and cut him with their swords across the shin-bones, and left him fainting from pain and loss of blood.

After further inquiries, he told me that he thought some of the Prussians were still in the cellar; upon which I ordered my batman to load his musket, struck a light, and with a lantern proceeded to the cellar, where we found a Prussian soldier drunk, and lying in a pool of wine which had escaped from the casks he and his comrades had tapped. Upon seeing us, he, with an oath in German, made a thrust at my batman with his sabre, which was parried; in an instant we bound the ruffian, and brought him at the point of the bayonet into the presence of the poor farmer, who recognised him as one of the men who had outraged his unfortunate daughters, and who had afterward wounded him. We carried our prisoner to the provost-sergeant, who, in his turn, took him to the Prussian headquarters, where he was instantly shot.

During the memorable retreat of Napoleon from the Rhine to Fontainebleau, the Allies amounted to five times the number of the French. Though greatly outnumbered, yet there was unity of will and of purpose in the councils of Napoleon and his generals, which Schwartzenberg and Blücher failed to infuse into their troops. Wanting neither in alacrity nor in vigour when the glory of his country was concerned, Napoleon, with his handful of men, made supernatural efforts, taking advantage of every good position that presented itself, and attacking the enemy upon several points upon the same day.

Upon one occasion he had completely divided the Allies by his comprehensive and well-arranged operations. Napoleon, to effect this gigantic manoeuvre, took the bull by its horns, and accordingly fought the Battle of Château-Thierry. In this sanguinary battle the French Army succeeded in taking from the Prussians all their cannon and ammunition, and several thousand prisoners. After the battle, General Bélliard, who commanded the advanced posts, naturally took possession of the town of Château-Thierry; and on entering the principal street with his staff, beheld a most shocking and horrible spectacle.

The Prussians had committed every sort of cruelty during the period they occupied Château-Thierry prior to the battle, and the inhabitants of that place were driven to such a pitch of exasperation, that when the battle turned in favour of the French, the people acted in a most barbarous and cruel manner toward every Prussian, whether wounded or not, who fell into their hands.

The first thing which General Bélliard saw in entering the town was a group of infuriated women, their hands bathed in blood, brandishing the knives with which they were busily employed in killing the wounded soldiers. The general and his staff had great difficulty in putting a stop to this horrid scene. The women, more like furies than human beings, addressed the general, saying they had undergone horrible treatment from the Germans, who had not only pillaged them of everything they possessed, but had violated all the women, both young and old, and had killed their husbands in cold blood. "Yes, general," cried one of those furies, "I have begun this butchery, and I will end it!" and in his presence she plunged her knife into the heart of a poor prisoner.

★★

The French Army of the North had now withdrawn into the capital, and on the 30th of June the First Corps of the Allies crossed the Oise, the advanced cavalry being at Louvres, twelve miles from Paris; and the First Division at La Chapelle, in the neighbourhood of Senlis.

On the 1st of July the two Brigades of Guards, with the Third Division, were within five miles of Paris, their right resting on Le Bourget, their left extending to the Forest of Bondy, a position which had been previously occupied by the Prussians. As the First Brigade of Guards was passing to the front to take the advanced posts, the Prussians formed up and gave a cheer, which was responded to enthusiastically by the British Guardsmen—a scene that was somewhat disheartening to the troops of Davoust's corps occupying Montmartre. During this march Lord Saltoun continued in temporary of the Second Battalion.

The duke took up his headquarters at Gonesse, halfway between Louvres and St. Denis, on the 2nd of July, and remained there three days, during which very little alteration was made in the position of the allied troops, except that the villages of Asnières, Courbevoie, and Suresnes were occupied by detachments of the duke's army, completing with the Prussians the investment of the north and west of Paris.

On the 4th the duke, in conjunction with Blücher, concluded a military convention with the French authorities, whereby the troops of France were to evacuate St. Denis and Neuilly the same day, the heights of Montmartre on the 5th, and Paris itself and on the 6th of July the Anglo-Allied troops took possession of the barriers to the north of the Seine, while the Prussians possessed the barriers to the south.

The Allies entered Paris on the 7th of July. The British troops encamping in the Bois de Boulogne. The Guards were to have marched through the streets with laurels in their caps, but at the last moment the authorities directed them to march straight to the "Bois," a quiet way of entering the capital not at all appreciated by either officers or men.

★★

I propose giving my own impression of the aspect of Paris and its vicinity when our regiment entered that city on the 25th of June, 1815. I recollect we marched from the plain of St. Denis, my battalion being about five hundred strong, the survivors of the heroic fight on the 18th of June. We approached near enough to be within fire of the batteries of Montmartre, and bivouacked for three weeks in the Bois de Boulogne. That now-beautiful garden was at the period to which I refer a wild, pathless wood, swampy, and entirely neglected. The Prussians, who were in bivouac near us, amused themselves by doing as much damage as they could, without any useful aim or object: they cut down the finest trees, and set the wood on fire at several points. There were about three test trees, and set the wood on fire at several points. There were about three thousand of the Guards then encamped in the wood, and I should think about ten thousand Prussians. Our camp was not remarkable for its courtesy toward them; in fact, our intercourse was confined to the most ordinary demands of duty, as Allies in an enemy's country.

I believe I was one of the first of the British Army who penetrated into the heart of Paris after Waterloo. I entered by the Porte Maillot, and passed the Arc de Triomphe, which was then building. In those days the Champs Elysees only contained a few scattered houses, and the roads and pathways were ankle-deep in mud. The only attempt at lighting was the suspension of a few lamps on cords which crossed the roads. Here I found the Scotch regiments bivouacking; their peculiar uniform created a considerable sensation amongst the Parisian women, who did not hesitate to declare that the want of *culottes* was most indecent. I passed through the camp, and proceeded on toward the garden of the Tuileries. This ancient palace of the kings of France presented, so far as the old front is concerned, the same aspect that it does at the present day; but there were then no flower-gardens, although the same stately rows of trees which now ornament the grounds were then in their midsummer verdure.

Being in uniform, I created an immense amount of curiosity amongst the Parisians; who, by the way, I fancied regarded me with no loving looks. The first house I entered was a *café* in the garden of the Tuileries, called Legac's. I there met a man who told me he was by descent an Englishman, though he had been born in Paris, and had really never quitted France. He approached me, saying, "Sir, I am delighted to see an English officer in Paris, and you are the first I have yet met with." He talked about the Battle of Waterloo, and gave me some useful directions concerning restaurants and *cafés*.

Along the boulevards were handsome houses, isolated, with gardens interspersed, and the roads were bordered on both sides with stately, spreading trees, some of them probably a hundred years old. There was but an imperfect pavement, the stepping-stones of which were adapted to display the Parisian female ankle and boot in all their calculated coquetry; and the road showed nothing but mother earth, in the middle of which a dirty gutter served to convey the impurities of the city to the river. The people in the streets appeared sulky and stupefied: here and there I noticed groups of the higher classes evidently discussing the events of the moment.

How strange humanity would look in our day in the costume of the first empire. The ladies wore very scanty and short skirts, which left little or no waist; their bonnets were of exaggerated proportions, and protruded at least a foot from their faces; and they generally carried a fan. The men wore blue or black coats, which were baggily made, and reached down to their ankles; their hats were enormously large, and spread out at the top.

I dined the first day of my entrance into Paris at the Café Anglais, on the Boulevard des Italiens; where I found, to my surprise, several of my brother officers. I recollect the charge for the dinner was about one-third what it would be at the present day. I had a potage, fish—anything but fresh, and, according to English predilections and taste, of course I ordered beefsteak and *pommes de terre*. The wine, I thought, was sour. The dinner cost about two *francs*.

The theatres at this time, as may easily be imagined, were not very well attended. I recollect going to the Français, where I saw for the first time the famous Talma. There was but a scanty audience; in fact, all the best places in the house were empty.

It may easily be imagined that, at a moment like this, most of those who had a stake in the country were pondering over the great and real drama that was then taking place. Napoleon had fled to Rochfort; the wreck of his army had retreated beyond the Loire; no list of killed and wounded had appeared; and, strange to say, the official journal of Paris had made out that the great Imperial Army at Waterloo had gained a victory. There were, nevertheless, hundreds of people in Paris who knew to the contrary, and many were already aware that they had lost relations and friends in the great battle.

Louis XVIII. arrived, as well as I can remember, at the Tuileries on the 26th of July, 1815, and his reception by the Parisians was a singular illustration of the versatile character of the French nation, and the sudden and often inexplicable changes which take place in the feeling of the populace. When the Bourbon, in his old lumbering state-carriage, drove down the boulevards, accompanied by the *Garde du Corps*, the people in the streets and at the windows displayed the wildest joy, enthusiastically shouting *"Vive le roi!"* amidst the waving of hats and handkerchiefs, while white sheets or white rags were made to do the duty of a Bourbon banner.

The king was dressed in a blue coat with a red collar, and

wore also a white waistcoat, and a cocked hat with a white cockade in it. His portly and good-natured appearance seemed to be appreciated by the crowd, whom he saluted with a benevolent smile.

I should here mention that two great devotees of the Church sat opposite to the king on this memorable occasion. The *cortège* proceeded slowly down the Rue de la Paix until the Tuileries was reached, where a company of the Guards, together with a certain number of the *Garde Nationale* of Paris, were stationed.

It fell to my lot to be on duty the day after, when the Duke of Wellington and Lord Castlereagh arrived to pay their respects to the restored monarch. I happened to be in the *Salle des Maréchaux* when these illustrious personages passed through that magnificent apartment. The respect paid to the Duke of Wellington on this occasion may be easily imagined, from the fact that a number of ladies of the highest rank, and of course partisans of the legitimate dynasty, formed an avenue through which the hero of Waterloo passed, exchanging with them courteous recognitions. The king was waiting in the grand reception apartment to receive the great British captain. The interview, I have every reason to believe, was not confined to the courtesies of the palace.

The position of the duke was a difficult one. In the first place, he had to curb the vindictive vandalism of Blücher and his army, who would have levelled the city of Paris to the ground, if they could have done so; on the other hand, he had to practise a considerable amount of diplomacy toward the newly restored king. At the same time, the duke's powers from his own government were necessarily limited. A spirit of vindictiveness pervaded the restored court against Napoleon and his adherents, which the duke constantly endeavoured to modify. I must not forget to give an illustration of this state of feeling.

It was actually proposed by Talleyrand, Fouché, and some important ecclesiastics of the ultra-royalist party, to arrest and shoot the Emperor Napoleon, who was then at Rochfort. So anxious were they to commit this criminal, inhuman, and cowardly act, on an illustrious fallen enemy, who had made the arms of France glorious throughout Europe, that they suggested to the duke, who had the command of the old wooden-armed semaphores, to employ the telegraph to order what I should have designated by no other name than the assassination of the Caesar of modern history.

★★★

Louis XVIII. made his public entry into Paris on the 8th, the same day that Napoleon set sail from Rochefort. Two days later, falling in with the English fleet, the deposed emperor yielded himself up to Captain Maitland, commanding the *Bellerophon*. Captain Maitland brought his prisoner to Torbay on the 24th, whereupon the British Government decreed that he should be conveyed to St. Helena without landing in England. He died on the island six years later in 1821.

★★★

A day or two after our arrival in Paris from Waterloo, Colonel Felton Hervey having entered the dining-room with the despatches which had come from London, the duke asked, "What news have you, Hervey?" upon which Colonel Hervey answered, "I observe by the *Gazette* that the Prince Regent has made himself Captain-General of the Life Guards and Blues, for their brilliant conduct at Waterloo."

"Ah!" replied the duke, "His Royal Highness is our sovereign, and can do what he pleases; but this I will say, the cavalry of other European armies have won victories for their generals, but mine have invariably got me into scrapes. It is true that they have always fought gallantly and bravely, and have generally got themselves out of their difficulties by sheer pluck."

The justice of this observation has since been confirmed by the charge at Balaklava, where our cavalry undauntedly rushed into the face of death under the command of that intrepid officer Lord Cardigan.

Also, by way of contrast, when we were in Paris, we heard that Napoleon, on making his first observation with his glass, surrounded by his generals, on the morning of the 18th, had said, with an air of exultation on finding that we had not retreated as he expected, *"Je les tiens donc ces Anglais;"* but was answered by General Foy, *"Sire, l'infanterie anglaise en duel c'est le diable."* We also heard that Soult, on remonstrating upon the uselessness of charging our squares with cavalry, had been severely reprimanded, and had undergone the biting and sarcastic remark from the emperor: *"Vous croyez Wellington un grand homme, général, parce qu'il vous a battu."*

About three weeks after the Battle of Waterloo I received orders from the Horse Guards to join my battalion in London. Two of my brother officers who had gone over to Paris, Tom Brooke and Hunter, the adjutant, who were to accompany me, requested me to return by way of Brussels, as they were very anxious to see the field of Waterloo. I complied with their request, and acted as their *cicerone*. On the following day we arrived in Brussels, and dined, a few days afterward, with General Sir George Cooke, who had commanded our division, and lost an arm. He was still suffering from his wound, and was living at the hotel where supper had been ordered for the Emperor Napoleon in anticipation of his certain triumph on the 18th.

Sir George observed to us that it was lucky for Lord Uxbridge that the field had been won by us; for had this not been the case, he would have got into an awkward scrape for having engaged the cavalry without orders from the duke. From what Sir George seemed to think, it was evidently the duke's intention to keep the cavalry in hand, and perfectly fresh, so that they might have charged the French squadrons when the latter had exhausted themselves in their attacks on our squares. To corroborate this opinion, he told us an anecdote of the war in Spain, which may be interesting, as showing how opposed the duke was to the harum-scarum custom of our cavalry officers, who hurled their men at full gallop on the enemy, without supports and without any actual plan or intimation beyond the ardour of a sportsman going at a five-barred gate.

He stated, when Sir Stapleton Cotton went out to take the command of the cavalry, at his first interview with Lord Wellington, his chief addressed him as follows:

"General Cotton, I am glad to see you in command of the cavalry; and I wish you to bear in mind that cavalry should be always. held well in hand; that your men and horses should not be used up in wild and useless charges, but put forward when you are sure that their onset will have a decisive effect. Above all, remember that you had better not engage, as a general rule, unless you see an opportunity of attacking the French with a superior force. In Spain, the Germans, the 14th Light Dragoons, and perhaps the 12th, under Fred. Ponsonby, were the only regiments that knew their duty and did not get into scrapes of every description."

When I arrived in London to join my battalion, I never shall forget the reception I met with as I dashed up in a chaise and four to the door of Fenton's Hotel in St. James's Street. Very few men from the army had yet arrived in London, and a mob of about a thousand people gathered around the door as I got out in my old weather-beaten uniform, shaking hands with me, and uttering loud cheers.

I also recollect the capital English dinner old James, the well-known waiter, had provided to celebrate my return. *"Ce sont les beaux jours de la vie,"* few and far between in our chequered existence, and I confess that my memory wanders back to them with pleasure, and some regret to think that they can never more return.

★★

On receipt of the news of the severe losses sustained by the battalions of Guards, reinforcements were at once ordered out from the home battalions, for, besides the wounded, the Second Battalion had now lost by death, since the 15th of June, 82, and the Third Battalion 75 men.

Detachments from the three regiments, amounting to 660 men of which 228 were for the First Guards, embarked on the 28th of June, and joined their respective service battalions at Paris on the 19th of July. The detachment of the First Guards was under Lieutenant-Colonel Dawson West, while the other officers accompanied it, or joined at Paris on its arrival, to fill up the Waterloo casualties.

These detachments arrived in time to witness the review of the Prussian Guards, 13,000 strong, which took place in presence of the Allied Sovereigns on Saturday, the 22nd of July, and they took part on the following Monday, the 24th, in a review of the whole of the duke's army, 65,000 strong, including the two Brigades of British Guards. It was remarked at the first review, even by Englishmen, that the Prussian Guards were the finest troops they had ever seen, though the French had beaten them, and that the British could not show such a fine body. Whether the Duke of Wellington heard these observations or not does not appear, but, as the Prussian Guards were marching past and all were admiring them, he turned to one next to him and said, with a thorough appreciation of the British character, "Ah, but I will show you on Monday some men that can lick these fellows."

★★

In July, 1815, it was agreed by the sovereigns of Russia, Austria, Prussia, Bavaria, Würtemberg, and a host of petty German powers—who had become wonderfully courageous and enthusiastically devoted to England, a few hours after the Battle of Waterloo—that a grand review should be held on the plains of St. Denis, where the whole of the allied forces were to meet. Accordingly, at an early hour on a fine summer morning, there were seen issuing from the various roads which centre on the plains of St. Denis, numerous English, Russian, Prussian, and Austrian regiments of horse and foot, in heavy marching order, with their bands playing; and finally, a mass of men, numbering not less than two hundred thousand, took up their positions on the wide-spreading field.

About twelve o'clock, the Duke of Wellington, commander-in-chief of the Allied Army, approached, mounted on his favourite charger; and, strange as it may appear, on his right was observed a lady in a plain riding-habit, who was no other than Lady Shelley, the wife of the late Sir John Shelley. Immediately behind the duke followed the Emperors of Austria, and Russia; the Kings of Prussia, Holland, Bavaria, and Würtemberg; several German princes, and general officers—the whole forming one of the most illustrious and numerous staffs ever brought together. The Duke of Wellington, thus accompanied, took up his position, and began manoeuvring, with a facility and confidence which elicited the admiration of all the experienced soldiers around him. Being on duty near His Grace, I had an opportunity of hearing Prince Schwartzenberg say to the duke, "You are the only man who can so well play at this game." The review lasted two hours; then the men marched home to their quarters, through a crowd of spectators which included the whole population of Paris. The most mournful silence was observed throughout on the part of the French.

✶✶✶

The British Army remained encamped all the summer and autumn in the Bois de Boulogne and its neighbourhood, and it was while quartered there, that the Second and Third Battalions of the First Guards received the notification that H.RH. the Prince Regent, in the name of the sovereign had been pleased to direct that their regiment should henceforward be styled:

"The First or Grenadier Regiment of Foot Guards,"

In commemoration of having defeated the French Imperial Guard at Waterloo.

As the season advanced the weather became too for the duke's army, amounting to 70,000 men and horses, to remain longer under canvas, but the quarters required for them, *viz.*, Versailles, St. Cloud, Sèvres, St. Germain, and others, were at the

THE BRITISH CAMP IN PARIS, 1815

time occupied by the Prussians; and it was not without some difficulty that, at the beginning of November, these were prevailed upon to make room for the British, Hanoverian, Dutch, and Belgic troops. On the 3rd of that month, however, the duke's army broke up its encampment, and was distributed in the above towns, with the exception of the division of Guards under Maitland, which came into Paris. A report was current that the reason of the British being kept so much longer under canvas, was a wish of the Duke of Wellington to display the greater hardihood of his troops.

★★★

It is only just to say that the moderation shown by the British Army, from the Duke of Wellington down to the private soldier, during our occupation of Paris, contrasted most favourably with that of the Russian and Prussian military. Whilst we simply did our duty, and were civil to all those with whom we came in contact, the Russians and Prussians were frequently most insubordinate, and never lost an opportunity of insulting a people whose armies had almost always defeated them on the day of battle.

I remember one particular occasion, when the Emperor of Russia reviewed his *Garde Impériale*, that the Cossacks actually charged the crowd, and inflicted wounds on the unarmed and inoffensive spectators. I once saw a regiment of Prussians march down the Rue St. Honoré when a line of half a dozen hackney coachman were quietly endeavouring to make their way in a contrary direction; suddenly some of the Prussian soldiers left their ranks, and with the butt-end of their muskets knocked the poor coachmen off their seats. I naturally felt ashamed at what I had seen, and being in uniform, some Frenchmen came up to me and requested me to report what I had witnessed to the Duke of Wellington. Upon my telling them it would be of no avail, they one and all said the English ought to blush at having Allies and friends capable of such wanton brutality.

The Duke of Wellington's conduct to the Parisians was kind and considerate. He contented himself with occupying the Bois de Boulogne, the two *faubourgs* of La Villette and La Chapelle St. Denis. Blücher was not so moderate in his conduct toward the French. His troops were billeted in every house; he obliged the inhabitants to feed and clothe them; and he issued an order (which I well recollect seeing) commanding the authorities to supply each soldier with a bedstead containing a bolster, a woollen mattress, two new blankets, and a pair of linen sheets. The rations per day, for each man, were two pounds of bread of good quality, one pound of butcher's meat, a bottle of wine, a quarter of a pound of butter, *ditto* rice, a glass of brandy, and some tobacco. The Prussian cavalry were not forgotten: each horse required ten pounds of oats, six of hay, *ditto* of straw, to be furnished early each day. Blücher's generals occupied all the best hotels in the Faubourg St. Germain; General Thielman that of Marshal Ney, where he forcibly took possession of the plate, carriages, and horses. Other Prussian generals acted in a similar manner.

The Russian and Austrian emperors imitated Blücher in some respects; they refused to quarter their soldiers in the large and wholesome barracks which were in readiness to receive them: no; they preferred billeting them with peaceable merchants and tradespeople, whom they plundered and bullied in the most outrageous manner. Wellington, all this while, showed great moderation, and his army paid for everything they required. Blücher, on the other hand, threatened to take possession of the Bank of France and the government offices, which threat was not carried into execution, owing to the wise and timely interposition of the duke.

One day, I recollect, Paris was in a state of amazement and stupefaction. Muffling, the commander-in-chief in Paris of the Prussians, installed at the Hotel de Ville, demanded from the French prefect a very large sum of money, and sent an officer and a hundred soldiers to enforce his demand. The prefect had not the money. The consequence was, he was marched off to the Hotel de Ville, where General Muffling kept him prisoner, intending, the following morning, to send him to Berlin as a hostage until the money was paid into the Prussian treasury.

The French had behaved so ill at Berlin, after the Battle of Jena, in 1806, that the Prussians had sworn to be revenged, if ever they had the opportunity to visit upon France the cruelties, the extortion, insults, and hard usage their own capital had suffered; and they kept their word.

One afternoon, when upwards of a hundred Prussian officers entered the galleries of the Palais Royal, they visited all the shops in turn, insulting the women and striking the men, breaking the windows, and turning everything upside down: nothing, indeed, could have been more outrageous than their conduct. When information was brought to Lord James Hay of what was going on, he went out, and arrived just as a troop of French *gendarmes* were on the point of charging the Prussians, then in the garden. He lost no time in calling out his men, and placing himself between the *gendarmes* and the officers, said he should fire upon the first who moved. The Prussians then came to him and said, "We had all vowed to return upon the heads of the French in Paris the insults that they had heaped upon our countrymen in Berlin; we have kept our vow, and we will now retire." Nothing could equal the bitter hatred which existed, and still exists, between the French and the Prussians.

Marshal Blücher, though a very fine fellow, was a very rough diamond, with the manners of a common soldier. On his arrival in Paris, he went every day to the *salon*, and played the highest stakes at *rouge-et-noir*. The *salon*, during the time that the marshal remained in Paris, was crowded by persons who came to see him play. His manner of playing was anything but gentleman-like, and when he lost, he used to swear in German at everything that was French, looking daggers at the croupiers. He generally managed to lose all he had about him, also all the money his servant, who was waiting in the antechamber, carried.

I recollect looking attentively at the manner in which he

played: he would put his right hand into his pocket, and bring out several *rouleaus* of *napoleons*, throwing them on the red or the black. If he won the first *coup*, he would allow it to remain; but when the croupier stated that the table was not responsible for more than ten thousand *francs*, then Blücher would roar like a lion, and rap out oaths in his native language which would doubtless have met with great success at Billingsgate, if duly translated; fortunately, they were not heeded, as they were not understood by the lookers-on.

A sort of congress of the Emperors of Austria and Russia and the King of Prussia, with Blücher and-Wellington, met at the Hotel of Foreign Affairs, on the Boulevard, when, after much ado, the Duke of Wellington emphatically declared that if any of the monuments were destroyed, he would take the British Army from Paris; this threat had the desired effect.

When Blücher was meditating the destruction of the bridge of Jena by blowing it up with powder, one of the old generals of the Empire proceeded to the Tuileries, saw the king, and mentioned what the Prussians intended doing. Louis, enraged, cried out, "What vandalism! I will place myself on the bridge and be blown up with it, rather than so fine a monument should be destroyed." The king then sent the Duc de Guiche to mention to the Duke of Wellington what had been communicated to him, upon which our illustrious chief ordered his horse, and, galloping off to the Guards' bivouacs in the Bois de Boulogne, gave directions to Sir P. Maitland to drive the Prussians off the bridge at the point of the bayonet, *coûte que coûte.* The Guards, on approaching the bridge, found the Prussian engineers hard at work undermining; but on discovering we were bent on mischief, and that our firelocks were loaded with ball cartridge—only five minutes being given them to remove all their pickaxes and other implements—they quietly marched off, to the great mortification of the officer in command, and to the disgust of Marshal Blücher, who never forgave Wellington for thwarting his purpose.

Nevertheless, Blücher levied contributions on the poor Parisians, and his army was newly clothed. The Bank of France was called upon to furnish him with several thousand pounds, which, it was said, were to reimburse him for the money lost at play. This, with many other instances of extortion and tyranny, was the cause of Blücher's removal, and he took his departure by order of the king.

★★

The internal affairs of France and the state of Europe generally becoming more settled towards the end of the year, a treaty was signed on the 20th of November, whereby it was agreed to remove a considerable portion of the several foreign armies then upon French territory, while the remainder should form an army of occupation in the country for the space of three years, (five years was first named), under the supreme command the Duke of Wellington.

Cambrai was fixed upon as the headquarters of the British Army, but the other stations were not then definitively settled; they were all, however, to be in the *Department du Nord*. Of the British troops then in Paris and its neighbourhood, three regiments of Household Cavalry, seven other cavalry regiments, the Second Battalions of Grenadier and Third Guards, and twenty-eight battalions of the Line, in all ten regiments of cavalry and thirty battalions, as well as five battalions still in Flanders, amounting altogether to 25,000 men, were selected to return home, and they proceeded accordingly to England at the beginning of December. The Second Battalion Grenadier Guards was at Abbeville, on its march home, on Christmas Day. There remained in France as the British Army of occupation nine regiments of cavalry, two battalions of Guards, and twenty-four battalions of the Line. This reduced army was divided into one corps of cavalry under Lord Combermere and one corps of infantry under Lord Hill.

As a fitting termination to the year 1815, it may be here recorded that, on the 23rd of December, the Prince Regent was pleased to approve of the Grenadier Guards being permitted to bear on their colours and appointments word "Waterloo," in commemoration of the distinguished services of the Second and Third Battalions of that regiment on the 18th of June, 1815.

An Afterword

As I advance in years, I find myself often wandering back to the scenes of my youth, and living over again the stirring events of my early days; and I confess to feeling a patriotic pride when I call to remembrance the glorious field of Waterloo—that "battle of giants," which decided the fate of the world. Many eloquent pages have been written on that stirring topic, and varied have been the accounts of that tremendous conflict; our present brave Allies to this very day continue to assert that they were not beaten, but were victims of a mistaken order, an act of treachery, or an evil destiny—in short, that they succumbed to anything but the genius of Wellington, the energy of Blücher, and the dauntless courage of the English and Prussian Armies.

I must say that I cannot understand how French writers imagine that they lessen the humiliation of defeat by attempting to decry or diminish the fame and prowess of the victor; or why M. Thiers and others, in their accounts of Waterloo, make so many vain attempts to prove that we ought to have lost the battle.

The Napoleon of M. Thiers's romance of Waterloo—it is certainly not a history—his Napoleon, I say, is not Napoleon as he was, but an ideal hero, omniscient and unerring. Ney and the other French generals are represented as brave blunderers, who could neither give, obey, nor execute an order; Wellington as a genius of the second-rate order, slow and unenterprising, and the English soldiers as fellows stubborn enough, but incapable of any aggressive movement—heavy, beef-fed knaves, standing up like logs, to be sabred, shot, and stuck by the active and intelligent veterans of the *Garde Imperiale*.

Thiers has been liberal to us in one respect. He has endowed several of our regiments with a very strong development of the vital principle. Many of our battalions, which, according to this great historian, had been entirely cut to pieces by the charges of French cavalry, nevertheless come to life again toward the end of M. Thiers's account of the engagement, and join with the utmost ardour in the last charge against the retreating French.

All this is quite unworthy of a great writer and statesman like M. Thiers, who has had every means of knowing the truth; and I, for one, cannot refrain from entering my protest against the innumerable errors, false assertions, and convenient suppressions contained in the twentieth volume of his history. The fame of Wellington, as one of the great captains of the age, is world-wide, and, written as it is on fifty fields of battle, needs no defence from me; but, when I hear the British soldier pooh-poohed and decried by M. Thiers, "who never set a squadron in the field, nor the division of a battle knew," I am moved to say a few words more on this stirring subject.

In spite of "*Les Victoires et Conquêtes de l'Armée Française*," I maintain that the British infantry is the finest in the world. I never saw anything to equal our old Peninsular regiments, not only for stubborn endurance, but for dash, pluck, intelligence, and skill in manoeuvring. Nothing could beat them; and if we had had the army of veterans with which we crossed the Bidassoa, on the field of Waterloo, we should have attacked the French instead of waiting their onset. But we had only twelve thousand of our old Peninsular infantry, the rest were raw troops; and though many did their best, they were hardly a match for the French Army, which was a very efficient one, and almost entirely composed of veterans.

When I call to mind how ill rewarded our noble soldiers were for their heroic deeds, my heart bleeds for them. "Under the cold shade of aristocracy," men who in France would have been promoted for their valour to the highest grades of the army, lived and died, twenty or thirty years after the battle, with the rank of lieutenant or captain. As to the private soldiers, their stubborn endurance, their desperate courage, their indomitable pluck, were but ill rewarded by a shilling or two a day, and a refuge in Chelsea or Kilmainham Hospital.

The late Mr. Creevey, the well-known Whig M.P., stated in my presence, at a dinner at Lord Darnley's, in Berkeley Square, in 1816, that he was at the Duke of Wellington's quarters at Brussels the night of the Battle of Waterloo. It was late when the duke entered, and, perceiving Mr. Creevey, shook him by the hand, and said, "I have won the greatest battle of modern times with twelve thousand of my old Peninsular troops."

Creevey remarked that he was astonished at that, and asked, "What, sir, with twelve thousand only?"

"Yes, Creevey," replied the duke; "with twelve thousand of my old Spanish infantry. I knew I could depend upon them. They fought the battle, without flinching, against immense odds; but nearly all my staff, and some of my best friends, are killed. Goodnight! I want rest, and must go to bed."

Creevey called at an early hour on the following morning, in the hope of again seeing the duke, but he had left Brussels before daylight, to join the army.

I do not pretend to say what the duke meant in his conversation with Mr. Creevey—who was truth itself—and I am equally certain that I am correctly relating what he said; for the statement made a great impression on me. He must have meant that the victory was mainly owing to the twelve thousand veterans; for, as near as I could make out, there were on our side at Waterloo about forty-five thousand English and Hanoverians, and twenty thousand Dutch, Belgian, and Nassau troops.

A Miscellany of Gronow's Military Anecdotes

MY SOLDIER SERVANT

When in Spain with my regiment, it fell to my lot to receive from the ranks a soldier born in Sicily, of Sicilian parentage, by named Proyd. When the Guards occupied Catania, this individual, having lost his father and mother, was adopted by the regiment, and through the instrumentality of Lord Proby became a soldier, and was inscribed on the muster-roll of the 1st Foot Guards. He was an excellent servant, and perhaps the best caterer in the army; for when we were invading the Pyrenees, he supplied me with every delicacy, while the army generally was living on salt beef and biscuits: in fact, poultry, mutton, and fresh bread at my table were the rule, rather than the exception. With all these accomplishments, he possessed one fault—a too great admiration, unqualified with respect, for the charms of the fair sex, and he seldom lost an opportunity of stealing a kiss from any pretty girl that came in his way.

On our return from the Peninsula, I took this figaro with me to White Knights, the seat of the Duke of Marlborough, where I was invited to spend some days. At this charming house I found a great number of visitors, among whom were Lord and Lady Grenville, Lord and Lady Macclesfield, Mr. Mathias, the author of the *Pursuits of Literature*, Lord William Fitzroy, Mr. Garlick, and others. It happened on the day of my arrival that my servant met the maid of Lady Macclesfield on the staircase, and without the slightest ceremony he attempted to kiss her. The maid, unaccustomed to such behaviour, screamed, ran downstairs, and then up again, with Proyd close at her heels; he even followed her into her lady's room, where she flew to take refuge. Her Ladyship, alarmed at seeing a strange man in her room, shrieked loudly; many persons ran to her assistance, and her noble husband, more dead than alive, thinking some sad disaster had befallen the countess, inquired with caution, "What is the matter?"

Her Ladyship replied, in a faint voice, "The man is under the bed."

Pokers and tongs were seized, and the noble lord made use of his weapons to such purpose that the delinquent quietly surrendered. This incident, which created great confusion, rendered it necessary that the Sicilian should be sent to rejoin his regiment. Poor Proyd soon after applied for his discharge, and returned to his native land to make love to his own countrywomen.

The Church Militant

I was acquainted, during the Peninsular War, with one of the army chaplains, the Rev. Mr. Frith, who was attached to the Fifth Division. He considered it part of his duty to attend the troops into action, and would frequently expose himself, with them, to the hottest fire. He showed the greatest courage and devotion, and rescued many wounded soldiers on several occasions, performing these, and many other gallant actions, as a matter of course and without any idea of display; for although a man of such remarkable bravery, he was of a quiet and gentle demeanour.

I remember on one occasion being present when a party of staff officers were trying to find a ford for the passage of a deep and rapid stream by a part of the army; most of the horses refused the water, when the reverend gentleman pushed forward, saying, "I dare say my nag will take it," and he was in a few minutes over on the other side and back again. Mr. Frith went by the name of "the fighting parson" in his division, and was an admirable and excellent specimen of the Church militant.

A Daring Exploit

Among the incidents that occurred in the war in Spain, the following will no doubt surprise the reader. In Picton's division in the Pyrenees, there was an Irishman of extraordinary courage, by name O'Keefe, who was addicted to all sorts of irregularities, which brought him more than once to the halberds, but who performed a feat worthy of the heroes of antiquity. Near the pass of Roncesvalles, the French occupied a peak or impregnable mountain called the Boar's Head, at the top of which a company of the enemy was posted. To drive them away appeared impossible; Picton thought so, and determined to invest this natural fort, to prevent useless bloodshed.

During a reconnaissance, the general said, in a loud voice, which was overheard by the men below, that the French could, if they pleased, pelt us away with stones from the top of the mountain. O'Keefe stepped up, touched his cap, and addressed Sir T. Picton thus: "If Your Honour chooses, I will take the hill alone."

The speech astonished all who heard it, but not the general, who had frequently witnessed the daring and intrepidity of O'Keefe. "If you do so," replied Sir Thomas, "I will report it to Lord Wellington, and I promise you your discharge, with a shilling a day for life."

O'Keefe stole away, having whispered to the commanding officer of his company to follow him, and climbed up the goat-path, the English sentinels firing at him, thinking he was deserting to the enemy. O'Keefe, having entered the stronghold of the French, was received with open arms, as a deserter. He then began to play his part, by showing signs of imbecility, laughing, dancing, singing, etc.; so that the enemy thought that they had actually received a madman instead of a deserter, and told him to decamp, as there was not food enough there to feed him.

During this farce, our men quickly got up to the summit, where they found O'Keefe occupying the attention of the enemy. They rushed in and took possession of this stronghold without losing a man. O'Keefe (I believe that was his name) received for this act of daring the nomination of one of the warders of the Tower from the Duke of Wellington.

Marshal Excelmann's Opinion of the British Cavalry

Experience has taught me that there is nothing more valuable than the opinions of intelligent foreigners on the military and naval excellences, and the failures, of our united service. Marshal Excelmann's opinion about the British cavalry struck me as remarkably instructive; he used to say:

"Your horses are the finest in the world, and your men ride better than any Continental soldiers; with such materials, the English cavalry ought to have done more than has ever been accomplished by them on the field of battle. The great deficiency is in your officers, who have nothing to recommend them but their dash and sitting well in their saddles; indeed, as far as my experience goes, your English generals have never understood the use of cavalry: they have undoubtedly frequently misapplied that important arm of a grand army, and have never, up to the Battle of Waterloo, employed the mounted soldier at the proper time and in the proper place. The British cavalry officer seems to be impressed with the conviction that he can dash and ride over everything; as if the art of war were precisely the same as that of fox-hunting. I need not remind you of the charge of your two heavy brigades at Waterloo: this charge was utterly useless, and all the world knows they came upon a masked battery, which obliged a retreat, and entirely disconcerted Wellington's plans during the rest of the day."

He added:

"Permit me to point out a gross error as regards the dress of your cavalry. I have seen prisoners so tightly habited that it was impossible for them to use their sabres with facility."

The French marshal concluded by observing:

"I should wish nothing better than such material as your men and horses are made of; since with generals who wield cavalry, and officers who are thoroughly acquainted with that duty in the field, I do not hesitate to say I might gain a battle."

Such was the opinion of a man of cool judgment, and one of the most experienced cavalry officers of the day.

The Duke at Carlton House

The Duke of Wellington dined frequently with the Prince Regent, who, when he had finished his iced punch and a bottle of sherry, began to be garrulous. The regent would invariably talk about the Battle of Waterloo, and speak of the way in which he had charged the French with the Household Brigade; upon one occasion he was so far gone that he had the temerity to tell the duke he had completely bowled over the French cavalry commanded by Marshal Ney. This was too much for the duke to swallow, and he said, "I have heard you, sir, say so before; but I did not witness this marvellous charge. Your Royal Highness must know that the French cavalry are the best in Europe."

At this same dinner Sir Watkyns William Wynn asked the illustrious duke whether he had a good view of the Battle of Waterloo, whereupon the baronet got the following laconic reply: "I generally like to see what I am about."

Sir John Elley

I have alluded to the extraordinary personal bravery of General Sir John Elley on the field of Waterloo, and his series of hand-to-hand encounters with the French cavalry on that great day. It is perhaps not generally known that this most distinguished officer commenced his career as a private in the Blues. He afterward commanded that celebrated regiment, for which he always had a great liking; and on a lengthened tour he once made through Europe, after the war, although a major-general, he always wore the uniform of the Royal Horse Guards.

When he arrived at Vienna, he was invited to dine at a full-dress dinner at the British ambassador's, on the occasion of King George IV.'s birthday. He was covered with orders, bestowed by the different sovereigns of Europe in 1815, and amongst these gorgeous ribands and crosses the modest Waterloo Medal appeared. Sir John happened to sit next to a French secretary of embassy, who criticised the English decoration, and said, "Surely, general, that is a very poor sort of order the government have given you and the other brave officers of the English Army. It cannot have cost them five *francs*."

"True," replied Sir John, making a low bow, "it has not cost our country more than five *francs*, but it cost yours a *napoleon*."

★★

In my former volumes I have had the pleasure of relating several anecdotes of this gallant officer; and in the third volume, I mentioned his having commenced his military career as a private in the Blues. I have received a letter from a gentleman, who knew him personally, giving me the following information respecting this dashing hero:

"I spent some time at Harrowgate with this gallant soldier, whom I admired not only for his bravery, but for his talents; he was replete with wit and fun, and full of the most interesting anecdotes. On my leaving him, he said that he had an old acquaintance residing not far from my father's place, whither I was going, and he would feel obliged if I would ride over some day to a certain toll-bar in the west of Cumberland, and deliver a message to his old friend, the sergeant who had enlisted him in the Blues.

"I did not forget a promise which might lead to some anecdotes respecting Sir John's early life, and shortly after arriving at home, I mounted my nag, rode to the toll-bar, and saw the old sergeant, who kept the turnpike and appeared to be seventy-five years of age. When he came to take the toll, he appeared much astonished at receiving the message from Sir John, and asking after his health, said that it was true that he had enlisted him into the Blues, and he related the circumstance: 'The sergeant having charge of a recruiting party at Barnet, one fine day a tall and respectable-looking young fellow addressed him, stating he wanted to enlist; the shilling was therefore given, and on the following day the recruit was sent to headquarters, where he was passed and duly enlisted in the Royal Guards.'"

The old man, being asked what he knew of Sir John's antecedents, said that the appearance and manner of the recruit proved him to have been a gentleman. He declined affirming as to the truth of what he had heard, but added that the report current in the regiment after his entering it, was that the new recruit had held a cornet's commission in the Scots Greys, then quartered at Doncaster, but owing to a misunderstanding with an officer about a lady, he had thrown up his commission in disgust, and having spent all his money, enlisted as a private in the manner described. In the barrack-room he was hail-fellow-well-met with all his comrades, who nevertheless treated him as their superior. As a swordsman and rider, he was considered the best in the regiment; and in consequence of his gentlemanly deportment, and being a good penman, he was taken into the adjutant's office, whence he was promoted to a commission in the regiment.

Perhaps the most distinguished service ever performed by Sir John Elley was in the cavalry engagement at the Battle of Vittoria, when he was assistant adjutant-general to the cavalry under the immediate command of Sir W. Cotton. Sir William had given directions to the 3rd Light Dragoons to charge a superior force of the enemy, which proved disastrous, for the regiment was almost entirely cut to pieces. Sir John Elley, observing this disaster, got together as many of the 14th and 16th Dragoons as he could, and charged at the head of them through the enemy; thereby saving many of the fine fellows who were dispersed and unable to act. In the charge he was knocked down, together with his horse, the fall breaking his leg; and although continually ridden over by friend and foe in the *mêlée*, Elley, nothing daunted, cheered on his men to fight for the honour of old England, and at last, catching hold of Sergeant Cooper's stirrup, was dragged to the rear.

The Emperor Alexander in Paris

The Emperor Alexander of Russia was fond of telling an anecdote of a circumstance which occurred to himself and the King of Prussia whilst in Paris in 1815. They had lounged together to the Palais Royal, which in those days was surrounded by a number of narrow streets and alleys, and, in returning to the Tuileries, they found that they were in a labyrinth, from which it was difficult to extricate themselves. The emperor, after a time, accosted a well-dressed man who wore the cross of St. Louis, and asked the nearest route to the Tuileries. The answer was, "I am going there myself, and will readily accompany you. Will you do me the honour of informing me who I am conducting?"

The *czar* replied, "I am the Emperor of Russia."

The gentleman received the information with an incredulous smile. "And who is your companion?" said he.

"This is the King of Prussia. But who am I to thank for this politeness?"

The Parisian, thinking that he would be a match for this waggish stranger, replied, "Oh, I am the Emperor of China."

Little further conversation passed between them, the Frenchman apparently declining to be further hoaxed. On their arrival at the gate of the Tuileries, however, the *générale* was beat, the soldiers saluted, and hats were taken off, to the amazement of the *soi-disant* monarch of the Celestial Empire, who was now convinced that his companions had higher claims to a throne than he possessed. When the two great personages turned around to thank their "guide, philosopher, and friend," they found that he also had assumed an *incognito*, and had disappeared.

Marshal Ney and Wellington

As an illustration of the false impressions which are always disseminated concerning public men, I must record the following fact: The Duke of Wellington was accused of being implicated in the military murder of Ney. Now, so far from this being the truth, I know positively that the Duke of Wellington used every endeavour to prevent this national disgrace; but the Church party, ever crafty and ever ready to profit by the weakness and passions of humanity, supported the king in his moments of excited revenge. It is a lamentable fact, but no less historical truth, that the Roman Catholic Church has ever sought to make the graves of its enemies the foundations of its power. The Duke of Wellington was never able to approach the king or use his influence to save Marshal Ney's life; but everything he could do was done, in order to accomplish his benevolent views. I repeat, the influence of the ultra-montane party triumphed over the Christian humanity of the illustrious duke.

Escape of Lavalette from Prison

Few circumstances created a greater sensation than the escape of Lavalette from the *conciergerie*, after he had been destined by the French Government to give employment to the guillotine. The means by which the prisoner avoided his fate and disappointed his enemies produced a deep respect for the English character, and led the French to believe that, however much the governments of France and England might be disposed to foster feelings either of friendship or of enmity, individuals could entertain the deepest sense of regard for each other, and that a chivalrous feeling of honour would urge them on to the exercise of the noblest feelings of our nature. This incident likewise had a salutary influence in preventing acts of cruelty and of bloodshed, which were doubtless contemplated by those in power.

Lavalette had been, under the Imperial Government, head of the post-office, which place he filled on the return of the

Bourbons; and when the Emperor Napoleon arrived from Elba, he continued still to be thus employed. Doubtless, on every occasion when opportunity presented itself, he did all in his power to serve his great master; to whom, indeed, he was allied by domestic ties, having married into the Beauharnais family.

When Louis the Eighteenth returned to Paris after the Battle of Waterloo, Lavalette and the unfortunate Marshal Ney were singled out as traitors to the Bourbon cause, and tried, convicted, and sentenced to death.

The 26th of December was the day fixed for the execution of Lavalette, a man of high respectability and of great connections, whose only fault was fidelity to his chief. On the evening of the 21st, Madame Lavalette, accompanied by her daughter and her governess, Madame Dutoit, a lady of seventy years of age, presented herself at the *conciergerie*, to take a last farewell of her husband. She arrived at the prison in a sedan-chair. On this very day the procureur-general had given an order that no one should be admitted without an order signed by himself; the *greffier* having, however, on previous occasions been accustomed to receive Madame Lavalette with the two ladies who now sought also to enter the cell, did not object to it, so these three ladies proposed to take coffee with Lavalette.

The under-gaoler was sent to a neighbouring *café* to obtain it, and during his absence Lavalette exchanged dresses with his wife. He managed to pass undetected out of the prison, accompanied by his daughter, and entered the chair in which Madame Lavalette had arrived; which, owing to the management of a faithful valet, had been placed so that no observation could be made of the person entering it. The bearers found the chair somewhat heavier than usual, but were ignorant of the change that had taken place, and were glad to find, after proceeding a short distance, that the individual within preferred walking home, and giving up the sedan to the young lady. On the *greffier* entering the cell, he quickly discovered the ruse, and gave the alarm; the under-gaoler was despatched to stop the chair, but he was too late.

Lavalette had formed a friendship with a young Englishman of the name of Bruce, to whom he immediately had recourse, throwing himself upon his generosity and kind feeling for protection, which was unhesitatingly afforded. But as Bruce could do nothing alone, he consulted two English friends who had shown considerable sympathy for the fate of Marshal Ney—men of liberal principles and undoubted honour, and both of them officers in the British service; these were Captain Hutchinson and General Sir Robert Wilson. To the latter was committed the most difficult task, that of conveying out of France the condemned prisoner; and for this achievement few men were better fitted than Sir Robert Wilson, a man of fertile imagination, ready courage, great assurance, and singular power of command over others, who spoke French well, and was intimately acquainted with the military habits of different nations.

Sir Robert Wilson's career was a singular one: he had commenced life an ardent enemy of Bonaparte, and it was upon his evidence, collected in Egypt and published to the world, that the great general was for a long time believed to have poisoned his wounded soldiers at Jaffa. Afterward he was attached to the allied sovereigns in their great campaign; but upon his arrival in Paris, his views of public affairs became suddenly changed, he threw off the yoke of preconceived opinions, became an ardent liberal, and so continued to the last hours of his life. The cause of this sudden change of opinion has never been thoroughly known, but certain it is that on every occasion he supported liberal opinions with a firmness and courage that astonished those who had known him in his earlier days.

Sir Robert undertook, in the midst of great dangers and difficulties, to convey Lavalette out of France. Having dressed him in the uniform of an English officer, and obtained a passport under a feigned name, he took him in a cabriolet past the barriers as far as Compiegne, where a carriage was waiting for them. They passed through sundry examinations at the forti-fied towns, but fortunately escaped; the great difficulty be-ing that, owing to Lavalette's having been the director of the posts, his countenance was familiar to almost all the postmas-ters who supplied relays of horses. At Cambray three hours were lost, from the gates being shut, and at Valenciennes they underwent three examinations; but eventually they got out of France.

The police, however, became acquainted with the fact that Lavalette had been concealed in the Rue de Helder for three days, at the apartments of Mr. Bruce, and this enabled them to trace all the circumstances, showing that it was at the apartments of Hutchinson that Lavalette had changed his dress, and that he had remained there the night before he quitted Paris. The consequence was that Sir Robert Wilson, Bruce, and Hutchinson were tried for aiding the escape of a prisoner, and each of them was condemned to three months' imprisonment; the under-gaoler, who had evidently been well paid for services rendered, had two years' confinement allot-ted to him.

I went to see Sir Robert Wilson during his stay in the *con-ciergerie*—a punishment not very difficult to bear, but which marked him as a popular hero for his life. A circumstance, I re-member, made a strong impression on me, proving that, how-ever great may be the courage of a man in trying circumstanc-es, a trifling incident might severely shake his nerves. I was accompanied by a favourite dog of the Countess of Oxford's, which, being unaware of the high character of Sir Robert, or dissatisfied with his physiognomy, or for some good canine reason, took a sudden antipathy to him, and inserted his teeth into a somewhat fleshy part, but without doing much injury. The effect, however, on the general was extraordinary: he was most earnest to have the dog killed. I, being certain that the animal was in no way diseased, avoided obeying his wishes, and fear that I thus lost the good graces of the worthy man.

THREE HEROIC BROTHERS

Among my souvenirs of 1815 there is one that has always struck me as particularly touching in the annals of French gallantry and heroism, and which shows what men we had to contend with in Spain, Portugal, and Belgium. There were three brothers named Angelet, whose heroic deeds have not, to the best of my knowledge, been recorded in any of the memoirs of that time, and who all died or were mortally wounded on the bloody field of Waterloo.

The eldest brother started for the army as a conscript; he soon after rose to the rank of sergeant, and for many acts of daring he was raised to the rank of an officer in a regiment of the line. When in Spain he was made prisoner by the guerillas, and as he was on the point of being massacred, his life was saved by an English officer; but he was imprisoned on the Spanish pontoons, where he suffered great hardships. He contrived, however, with singular daring and dexterity, to make his escape.

Angelet went through the Russian campaign as captain in the Imperial Guard, was named major in the 141st Regiment in 1813, and took a glorious part in the Battle of Lützen, where he was dangerously wounded by a cannon-ball in the leg. After his recovery, he returned to the Imperial Guard with the rank of lieutenant-colonel, and was engaged in all the battles of 1814. On the return of the Bourbons, he was named colonel of the grenadiers of the *Garde Royale*; but, on the escape of Napoleon from Elba, he immediately joined his glorious chief. After many heroic deeds at Waterloo, he received five wounds, and died at Brussels, after lingering in great agony for two months. His last moments were soothed by the presence of a beautiful young girl, to whom he was engaged to be married when he left Paris to conquer or to die.

The second brother, St. Amand Angelet, was educated at the *École Militaire*, was present at almost every battle in Spain, and for his gallant deeds obtained the cross of the Legion of Honour (which was not then as easily won as it is nowadays) and the rank of captain. He received a wound in the leg at Orthes, and returned to Paris in 1814 to have it cured, though he was always obliged to go on crutches.

St. Amand was named to the regiment commanded by his brother, and had to endure all the insolence that Napoleon's brave soldiers were forced at that time to undergo from the titled young *blancbecs* set over them by the Bourbons. St. Amand had for his *chef de bataillon* a young *émigré* of eighteen, who had never seen a shot fired, was perfectly ignorant of all military science, and excelled only in the art of tormenting his inferiors in grade. On the return of the Emperor Napoleon, in 1815, St. Amand Angelet compelled this insolent aristocrat to eat his *croix du lys* (the order of the Bourbons), in order that it might meet with the most ignominious destiny.

Angelet, who was a very handsome and agreeable man, and very much the fashion, was one day in a salon of the Faubourg St. Germain openly expressing his joy at the emperor's return, when a great lady who was present jeered him on his inability, on account of his wounds, to do more than speak in favour of his hero. St. Amand, stung to the quick, and devoured by martial ardour and that passionate devotion for his chief which was the characteristic of every man in the French Army, started immediately for the frontier, and made the campaign of 1815 on his crutches. He was killed in the early part of the day at Waterloo.

The third brother, who was mild and gentle as a woman in face and manner, also fell bravely fighting in the last charge of that bloody day. After the battle, Doctor D——, an intimate friend of the Angelet family, went to announce to the bereaved mother, who was also a widow, the death of her two younger sons. The eldest was still lingering at Brussels. "I do not wish him to recover," said the weeping woman, "for then I should be forced to live for his sake, whereas when he goes, I may follow and join all those I have loved upon earth." She died in the course of the year of a broken heart—that malady which slays more than are numbered in the lists of men.

An Insult Rightly Redressed

Soon after the restoration of the Bourbons, several duels took place for the most frivolous causes. Duels were fought in the daytime, and even by night. The officers of the Swiss Guards were constantly measuring swords with the officers of the old *Garde Impériale*. Upon one occasion a Frenchman, determined to insult a Swiss officer, who, in the uniform of his regiment, was quietly taking his ice at Tortoni's, addressed him thus: "It would not serve my country for the sake of money as you do. We Frenchmen think only of honour."

To which the other promptly retorted, "You are right, for we both of us serve for what we do not possess."

A duel was the consequence; they fought with swords under a lamp in the Rue Taitbout, and the Frenchman was run through the body, but luckily the wound, though dangerous, did not prove fatal.

Duelling in France in 1815

When the restoration of the Bourbons took place, a variety of circumstances combined to render duelling so common, that scarcely a day passed without one at least of these hostile meetings. Amongst the French themselves there were two parties always ready to distribute to each other "*des coups d'épée*"—the officers of Napoleon's army and the Bourbonist officers of the *Garde du Corps*. Then, again, there was the irritating presence of the English, Russian, Prussian, and Austrian officers in the French capital. In the duels between these soldiers and the French, the latter were always the aggressors.

At Tortoni's, on the Boulevards, there was a room set apart for such quarrelsome gentlemen, where, after these meetings, they indulged in riotous champagne breakfasts. At this *café* might be seen all the most notorious duellists, amongst whom I can call to mind an Irishman in the *Garde du Corps*, W——, who was a most formidable fire-eater. The number of duels in which he had been engaged would seem incredible in the present day: he is said to have killed nine of his opponents in one year!

The Marquis de H——, descended of an ancient family in Brittany, also in the *Garde du Corps*, likewise fought innumerable duels, killing many of his antagonists. I have heard that on entering the army he was not of a quarrelsome disposition, but being laughed at and bullied into fighting by his brother officers, he, from the day of his first duel, like a wild beast that had once smelt blood, took a delight in such fatal scenes, and was ever ready to rush at and quarrel with anyone. The marquis has now, I am glad to say, subsided into a very quiet, placable, and peace-making old gentlemen; but at the time I speak of he was much blamed for his duel with F——, a young man of nineteen. While dining at a *café* he exclaimed, "*J'ai envie de tuer quelqu'un,*" and rushed out into the street and to the theatres, trying to pick a quarrel; but he was so well known that no one was found willing to encounter him. At last, at the Théâtre de la Porte St. Martin, he grossly insulted this young man, who was, I think, an *élève* of the *École Polytechnique*, and a duel took place, under the lamp-post near the theatre, with swords. He ran F—— through the body, and left him dead upon the ground.

The late Marshal St. A—— and General J—— were great duellists at this time, with a whole host of others whose names I forget. The meetings generally took place in the Bois de Boulogne, and the favourite weapon of the French was the small sword or the sabre; but foreigners, in fighting with the French, who were generally capital swordsmen, availed themselves of the use of pistols. The ground for a duel with pistols was marked out by indicating two spots, which were twenty-five paces apart; the seconds then generally proceeded to toss up who should have the first shot; the principals were then placed, and the word was given to fire.

The Café Foy, in the Palais Royal, was the principal place of rendezvous for the Prussian officers, and to this *café* the French officers on half-pay frequently proceeded in order to pick quarrels with their foreign invaders; swords were quickly drawn, and frequently the most bloody frays took place: these originated not in any personal hatred, but from national jealousy on the part of the French, who could not bear the sight of foreign soldiers in their capital, which, when ruled by the great captain of the age, had, like Rome, influenced the rest of the world. On one occasion, our Guards, who were on duty at the Palais Royal, were called out to put an end to one of these encounters, in which fourteen Prussians and ten Frenchmen were either killed or wounded.

The French took every opportunity of insulting the English, and very frequently, I am sorry to say, those insults were not met in a manner to do honour to our character. Our countrymen in general were very pacific; but the most awkward customer the French ever came across was my fellow countryman the late gallant Colonel Sir Charles S——, of the Engineers, who was ready for them with anything: sword, pistol, sabre, or fists—he was good at all; and though never seeking a quarrel, he would not put up with the slightest insult. He killed three Frenchmen in Paris, in quarrels forced upon him. I remember, in October, 1815, being asked by a friend to dine at Beauvillier's, in the Rue Richelieu, when Sir Charles S——, who was well known to us, occupied a table at the farther end of the room.

About the middle of the dinner, we heard a most extraordinary noise, and, on looking up, perceived that it arose from S——'s table; he was engaged in beating the head of a smartly dressed gentleman with one of the long French loaves so well known to all who have visited France. On being asked the reason of such rough treatment, he said he would serve all Frenchmen in the same manner if they insulted him. The offence, it seems, proceeded from the person who had just been chastised in so summary a manner, and who had stared and laughed at S—— in a rude way, for having ordered three bottles of wine to be placed upon his table. The upshot of this was a duel, which took place next day at a place near Vincennes, and in which S—— shot the unfortunate jester.

When Sir Charles returned to Valenciennes, where he

commanded the Engineers, he found on his arrival a French officer waiting to avenge the death of his relation, who had only been shot ten days before at Vincennes. They accordingly fought before S—— had time even to shave himself or eat his breakfast; he having only just arrived in his *coupé* from Paris. The meeting took place in the fosse of the fortress, and the first shot from S——'s pistol killed the French officer, who had actually travelled in the diligence from Paris for the purpose, as he boasted to his fellow travellers, of killing an Englishman.

A Captain B——, of one of our cavalry regiments quartered in that town, was insulted by a French officer. B—— demanded satisfaction, which was accepted; but the Frenchman would not fight with pistols. B—— would not fight with swords; so, at last it was agreed that they should fight on horseback, with lances. The duel took place in the neighbourhood of Beauvais, and a crowd assembled to witness it. B——received three wounds; but, by a lucky prod, eventually killed his man. B—— was a fine-looking man and a good horseman. My late friend the Baron de P——, so well-known in Parisian circles, was second to the Frenchman on this occasion.

MAJOR-GENERAL STEWART AND LORD WELLINGTON

If the present generation of Englishmen would take the trouble of looking at the newspaper which fifty years ago informed the British public of passing events both at home and abroad, they would, doubtless, marvel at the very limited and imperfect amount of intelligence which the best journals were enabled to place before their readers. The progress of the Peninsular campaign was very imperfectly chronicled; it will, therefore, be easily imagined what interest was attached to certain letters that appeared in the *Morning Chronicle*, which criticised with much severity, and frequently with considerable injustice, the military movements of Lord Wellington's Spanish campaigns.

The attention of the commander-in-chief being drawn to these periodical and personal comments on his conduct of the war, his lordship at once perceived, from the information which they contained, that they must have been written by an officer holding a high command under him. Determined to ascertain the author—who, in addressing a public journal, was violating the Articles of War, and, it might be, assisting the enemy,—means were employed in London to identify the writer. The result was that Lord Wellington discovered the author of the letters to be no other than Sir Charles Stewart, the late Lord Londonderry. As soon as Lord Wellington had made himself master of this fact, he summoned Sir Charles Stewart to headquarters at Torres Vedras; and, on his appearance, he, without the least preface, addressed him thus:

"Charles Stewart, I have ascertained with deep regret that you are the author of the letters which appeared in the *Morning Chronicle*, abusing me and finding fault with my military plans."

Lord Wellington here paused for a moment, and then continued:

"Now, Stewart, you know your brother Castlereagh is my best friend, to whom I owe everything; nevertheless, if you continue to write letters to the *Chronicle*, or any other newspaper, by God, I will send you home."

Sir Charles Stewart was so affected at this rebuke that he shed tears, and expressed himself deeply penitent for the breach of confidence and want of respect for the articles of war. They immediately shook hands and parted friends. It happened, however, that Sir Charles Stewart did not remain long in the cavalry, of which he was adjutant-general. Within a few weeks he was named one of the commissioners deputed to proceed to the allied armies, where the sovereigns were then completing their plans to crush Napoleon.

Sir John Waters

Amongst the distinguished men in the Peninsular War whom my memory brings occasionally before me, is the well-known and highly popular Quartermaster-General Sir John

Waters, who was born at Margam, a Welsh village in Glamorganshire. He was one of those extraordinary persons that seem created by kind nature for particular purposes; and without using the word in an offensive sense, he was the most admirable spy that was ever attached to an army. One would almost have thought that the Spanish war was entered upon and carried on in order to display his remarkable qualities. He could assume the character of Spaniards of every degree and station, so as to deceive the most acute of those whom he delighted to imitate.

In the *posada* of the village he was hailed by the contrabandist or the muleteer as one of their own race; in the gay assemblies he was an accomplished *hidalgo*; at the bull-fight the *toreador* received his congratulations as from one who had encountered the *toro* in the arena; in the church he would converse with the friar upon the number of *Ave Marias* and *Paternosters* which could lay a ghost, or tell him the history of every one who had perished by the flame of the Inquisition, relating his crime, whether carnal or anti-Catholic; and he could join in the *seguadilla* or in the *guaracha*.

But what rendered him more efficient than all was his wonderful power of observation and accurate description, which made the information he gave so reliable and valuable to the Duke of Wellington. Nothing escaped him. When amidst a group of persons, he would minutely watch the movement, attitude, and expression of every individual that composed it; in the scenery by which he was surrounded he would carefully mark every object: not a tree, not a bush, not a large stone, escaped his observation; and it was said that in a cottage he noted every piece of crockery on the shelf, every domestic utensil, and even the number of knives and forks that were got ready for use at dinner.

His acquaintance with the Spanish language was marvellous; from the finest works of Calderon to the ballads in the *patois* of every province, he could quote, to the infinite delight of those with whom he associated. He could assume any character that he pleased: he could be the Castilian, haughty and reserved; the Austrian, stupid and plodding; the Catalonian, intriguing and cunning; the Andalusian, laughing and merry; in short, he was all things to all men. Nor was he incapable of passing off, when occasion required, for a Frenchman; but as he spoke the language with a strong German accent, he called himself an Alsatian. He maintained that character with the utmost nicety, and as there is a strong feeling of fellow-ship, almost equal to that which exists in Scotland, amongst all those who are born in the departments of France bordering on the Rhine, and who maintain their Teutonic originality, he always found friends and supporters in every regiment in the French service.

He was on one occasion entrusted with a very difficult mission by the Duke of Wellington, which he undertook effectually to perform, and to return on a particular day with the information that was required.

Great was the disappointment when it was ascertained beyond a doubt that just after leaving the camp, he had been taken prisoner, before he had time to exchange his uniform. Such, however, was the case: a troop of dragoons had intercepted him and carried him off, and the commanding officer desired two soldiers to keep a strict watch over him and carry him to headquarters. He was of course disarmed, and being placed on a horse, was, after a short time, galloped off by his guards. He slept one night under durance vile at a small inn, where he was allowed to remain in the kitchen; conversation flowed on very glibly, and as he appeared a stupid Englishman who could not understand a word of French or Spanish, he was allowed to listen, and thus obtained precisely the intelligence that he was in search of. The following morning, being again mounted, he overheard a conversation between his guards, who deliberately agreed to rob him, and to shoot him at a mill where they were to stop, and to report to their officer that they had been compelled to fire at him in consequence of his attempt to escape.

Shortly before they arrived at the mill, for fear that they might meet with someone who would insist on having a portion of the spoil, the dragoons took from their prisoner his watch and his purse, which he surrendered with a good grace. On their arrival at the mill they dismounted, and in order to give some appearance of truth to their story, they went into the house, leaving their prisoner outside, in the hope that he would make some attempt to escape. In an instant Waters threw his cloak upon a neighbouring olive bush, and mounted his cocked hat on the top. Some empty flour sacks lay upon the ground, and a horse laden with well-filled flour sacks stood at the door. Sir John contrived to enter one of the empty sacks and throw himself across the horse. When the soldiers came out of the house they fired their carbines at the supposed prisoner, and galloped off at the utmost speed.

A short time after the miller came out and mounted his steed; the general contrived to rid himself of the encumbrance of the sack, and sat up, riding behind the man, who, suddenly turning round, saw a ghost, as he believed, for the flour that still remained in the sack had completely whitened his fellow traveller and given him a most unearthly appearance. The frightened miller was "putrified," as Mrs. Malaprop would say, at the sight, and a push from the white spectre brought the unfortunate man to the ground, when away rode the gallant quartermaster with his sacks of flour, which, at length bursting, made a ludicrous spectacle of man and horse.

On reaching the English camp, where Lord Wellington was anxiously deploring his fate, a sudden shout from the soldiers made his lordship turn round, when a figure, resembling the statue in "Don Juan," galloped up to him. The duke, affectionately shaking him by the hand, said:

"Waters, you never yet deceived me; and though you have come in a most questionable shape, I must congratulate you and myself."

When this story was told at the clubs, one of those listeners, who always want something more, called out, "Well, and what did Waters say?" to which Alvanley replied:

"Oh, Waters made a very *flowery* speech, like a well-bred man."

THE LATE DUKE OF RICHMOND

One of the most intimate friends of the Duke of Wellington was the Earl of March, afterward Duke of Richmond. He was a genuine hardworking soldier, a man of extraordinary courage, and one who was ever found ready to gain laurels amidst the greatest dangers. When the 7th Fusiliers crossed the Bidassoa, the late duke left the staff and joined the regiment in which he had a company. At Orthes, in the thick of the fight, he received a shot which passed through his lungs; from this severe wound he recovered sufficiently to be able to join the Duke of Wellington, to whom he was exceedingly useful, at the Battle of Waterloo. On his return to England, he united himself to the most remarkably beautiful girl of the day, the eldest daughter of Lord Anglesea, and whose mother was the lovely Duchess of Argyle.

WELLINGTON'S FIRST CAMPAIGN

The Duke of Wellington had in his early career lost a considerable sum of money at play, and had been on the point of selling his commission in Dublin, with the view of relieving himself from some debts of honour which he incurred.

At a dinner party at Mr. Greenwood's, of that excellent firm, Cox and Greenwood, I met Sir Harry Calvert, then Adjutant-General, who accompanied the Duke of York as one of his staff in his disastrous campaign in Holland; and he told us the following anecdote: Lord Camden, the Viceroy, had been applied to by Lord Mornington, the brother of Captain Wesley (so his name was then spelt), for a commissionership of customs, or anything else in the gift of the Lord Lieutenant of Ireland, as it was the intention of the captain to sell his commission to pay his debts. Lord Camden, in an interview with Captain Wesley, inquired whether he left the army in disgust, or what motive induced him to relinquish a service in which he was well qualified to distinguish himself. Captain Wesley explained everything that had occurred, upon which the lord lieutenant expressed a wish to be of service to him. "What can I do for you? Point out any plan by which you can be extricated from your present difficulties."

The answer was, "I have no alternative but to sell my commission, for I am poor, and unable to pay off my debts of honour."

"Remain in the army," said Lord Camden, "and I will assist you in paying off your liabilities."

"I should like to study my profession at Angers," replied the young soldier; "for the French are the great masters of the art of war."

Lord Camden assented to the proposition, supplied him with the means of living in France, and paid his debts.

Captain Wellesley, availing himself of the generous assistance thus offered, spent a considerable time at the Military School at Angers, where he laboured with intense application, and laid the foundation of that military reputation which placed him above all competitors. It was this education that enabled him to gain his first laurels. On his return to England, he was ordered to join the Duke of York in Flanders, as Major of the 33d Regiment of Foot; and the colonel and first major being absent, the command of the regiment devolved upon him. The expedition landed near Furnes in the Netherlands, the crack regiments first; and these, directly they set foot on shore, advanced helter-skelter, fancying themselves on the highroad to Paris.

When the 33rd disembarked, Major Wellesley, knowing French tactics, addressed himself to Captain Calvert, the Duke of York's *aide-de-camp*, pointing out the certainty of a speedy attack of the enemy's cavalry and artillery, and the great probability that every man who had advanced would be cut to pieces. He said, "Pray, allow me to form squares of divisions upon the beach before it is too late." This was done, and almost immediately afterward, Vandamme, with the whole of his cavalry, supported by artillery, came down, threatening to sweep everything before them. Our troops rapidly dispersing, luckily found the 33rd in square, and were thus saved from annihilation. The Duke of York observing this adroit and ready manoeuvre on the part of the young major, called him to his council, and gave him the command of the rear-guard. After continually fighting and retreating for several weeks, the army embarked for England.

The reputation thus gained led to Major Wellesley's appointment in India, where he displayed those abilities which marked him out as the only man to oppose, and finally to conquer, the greatest of modern generals.

The lesson the Duke of Wellington had learnt at the gambling-table, as a young man, was deeply impressed upon him: he never afterward touched a card; and so firmly did he set his face against gambling, that, in Paris, none of his staff, from Lord Fitzroy Somerset down to Freemantle, was ever to be seen either at Frascati's or the Salon des Étrangers.

www.ingramcontent.com/pod-product-compliance
Lightning Source LLC
Chambersburg PA
CBHW021055090426
42738CB00006B/346

* 9 7 8 1 9 1 6 5 3 5 4 7 3 *